# ITIL® 4 Drive Stakeholder Value (DSV)

Your companion to the ITIL 4 Managing Professional DSV certification

# ITIL® 4 Drive Stakeholder Value (DSV)

Your companion to the ITIL 4 Managing Professional DSV certification

CLAIRE AGUTTER

**IT Governance Publishing**

Every possible effort has been made to ensure that the information contained in this book is accurate at the time of going to press, and the publisher and the author cannot accept responsibility for any errors or omissions, however caused. Any opinions expressed in this book are those of the author, not the publisher. Websites identified are for reference only, not endorsement, and any website visits are at the reader's own risk. No responsibility for loss or damage occasioned to any person acting, or refraining from action, as a result of the material in this publication can be accepted by the publisher or the author.

ITIL® is a registered trade mark of AXELOS Limited. All rights reserved.

Apart from any fair dealing for the purposes of research or private study, or criticism or review, as permitted under the Copyright, Designs and Patents Act 1988, this publication may only be reproduced, stored or transmitted, in any form, or by any means, with the prior permission in writing of the publisher or, in the case of reprographic reproduction, in accordance with the terms of licences issued by the Copyright Licensing Agency. Enquiries concerning reproduction outside those terms should be sent to the publisher at the following address:

IT Governance Publishing Ltd
Unit 3, Clive Court
Bartholomew's Walk
Cambridgeshire Business Park
Ely, Cambridgeshire
CB7 4EA
United Kingdom
*www.itgovernancepublishing.co.uk*

© Claire Agutter 2022

The author has asserted the rights of the author under the Copyright, Designs and Patents Act, 1988, to be identified as the author of this work.

First edition published in the United Kingdom in 2022 by IT Governance Publishing

ISBN 978-1-78778-351-5

# ABOUT THE AUTHOR

Claire Agutter is a service management trainer, consultant and author. In 2020, she was one of Computer Weekly's Top 50 Most Influential Women in Tech. In 2018 and 2019, she was recognised as an HDI Top 25 Thought Leader and was part of the team that won itSMF UK's 2017 Thought Leadership Award. Claire provides regular, free content to the IT service management (ITSM) community as the host of the popular ITSM Crowd hangouts, and is the chief architect for VeriSM™, the service management approach for the digital age. Claire is the director of ITSM Zone, which provides online ITSM training, and Scopism. She has worked with IT Governance Publishing to publish *Service Integration and Management (SIAM™) Foundation Body of Knowledge (BoK), Second edition* and *Service Integration and Management (SIAM™) Professional Body of Knowledge (BoK), Second edition*, the official guides for the EXIN SIAM™ Foundation and Professional certifications.

After providing support to thousands of people taking ITIL training and certification from version 2 onwards, Claire has created this series of books for those studying towards ITIL 4 Managing Professional and Strategic Leader status.

**For more information, please visit:**

- *https://itsm.zone*
- *www.scopism.com*

**Contact:**

- *www.linkedin.com/in/claireagutter/*

*About the author*

**For more information about Claire's other publications with ITGP, visit:**

*www.itgovernancepublishing.co.uk/author/claire-agutter*

# CONTENTS

**Introduction** ..................................................................... 1
   How to use this book ................................................... 1
**Chapter 1: The customer journey** .................................. 5
   Value streams and customer journeys ........................... 5
   Customer journey design .............................................. 9
   Customer journey key concepts .................................. 10
   Designing and improving the customer journey ........... 19
**Chapter 2: Targeting markets and stakeholders** ......... 29
   Understanding markets ............................................... 29
   Market segmentation .................................................. 30
   Targeting markets ....................................................... 32
   Understanding customers and service providers .......... 38
**Chapter 3: Fostering stakeholder relationships** .......... 49
   Supplier and partner relationships ............................... 52
   Customer relationships ............................................... 66
   Analysing customer needs .......................................... 77
   The relationship management practice ........................ 83
   The supplier management practice .............................. 88
**Chapter 4: How to shape demand and define service offerings** ........................................................................ 93
   Designing digital service experiences ......................... 95
   Approaches for selling and obtaining service offerings ................................................................... 102
   Managing demand and opportunities ......................... 105
   Managing requirements ............................................ 114
   The business analysis practice .................................. 126
**Chapter 5: How to align expectations and agree service details** ............................................................. 131
   Value co-creation, negotiations and agreement ......... 134
   The service level management practice ..................... 145

*Contents*

**Chapter 6: Onboarding and offboarding** ...................151
    Onboarding, offboarding and user relationships..........153
    Planning onboarding and offboarding, user engagement ...............................................................160
    The service catalogue management practice................176
    The service desk practice .............................................180
**Chapter 7: Continual value co-creation**.......................189
    Fostering a service mindset..........................................192
    Service request and provision ......................................208
    The service request management practice ...................217
**Chapter 8: Realising and validating service value**......221
    Service and value measurement and validation...........223
    The portfolio management practice .............................248
**Chapter 9: Exam preparation**........................................253
**Appendix A: Banksbest case study**................................257
    Company overview ......................................................257
    Company structure .......................................................258
    Future plans..................................................................259
    IT services....................................................................259
    IT department...............................................................260
    IT service management................................................261
    Sample employee biographies .....................................261
**Further reading**..............................................................263

# INTRODUCTION

**How to use this book**

The majority of this book is based on the *ITIL 4 Drive Stakeholder Value* (DSV) publication and the associated ITIL 4 Specialist: Drive Stakeholder Value syllabus.

The *ITIL 4 Drive Stakeholder Value* publication describes *"the steps of co-creating value through services in significant detail and is beneficial to both customers and service providers"*. It explains how to *"optimize the value of the journey for all stakeholders, for example, to convert opportunity and demand into value and to drive stakeholder value"*.

The key themes related to driving stakeholder value and its supporting management practices are the focus of the DSV publication and associated training and examination.

In this companion publication to DSV, in addition to helping you prepare for your certification, I also want to give you advice and guidance that will lead to you using this book once your training and exam are complete. I've added my own practical experience and given you advice and points to think about along the way. My goal is for you to refer back to this book in years to come, not just put it away once you've passed your exam. With this additional content, you'll find this book is an excellent supplement to any training course and a useful tool in your ongoing career.

As you read the book, assume that all the content is related to the syllabus unless it is highlighted in one of two ways:

*Introduction*

> **Something for you:** an exercise for you to complete to apply the ITIL 4 concepts in your own role, or a point for you to think about. This content is not examinable.
>
> **Practical experiences:** any content marked out with this image is based on my own experience and is not examinable.

The content highlighted as something for you to think about or practical experience might also refer to the Banksbest case study you can find in Appendix A. I'll use the case study to give an example of how something would work in the real world, or to help you apply what you're reading about. Case studies can really help to bring abstract concepts to life. The case study is not examinable, but using it will help you get a deeper understanding of the DSV concepts you are learning.

Let's start with something for you now:

*Introduction*

> Why not read the case study and make a note of your first impressions of the Banksbest organisation and its plans before you start to study the DSV content in this book?

Unless stated otherwise, all quotations are from *ITIL® 4 Drive Stakeholder Value* and *Practice Guides* published by AXELOS in 2020. Copyright © AXELOS Limited 2020. Used under permission of AXELOS Limited. All rights reserved.

# CHAPTER 1: THE CUSTOMER JOURNEY

In this introductory chapter, we'll review a key concept for DSV – the customer journey. The content includes:

- The concept of the customer journey; and
- How to design and improve customer journeys.

ITIL 4 describes a customer journey as *"the complete end-to-end experience customers have with one or more service providers and/or their products through the touchpoints and service interactions"*.

**Value streams and customer journeys**

Figure 1 shows the relationships between value streams and customer journeys.

## 1: The customer journey

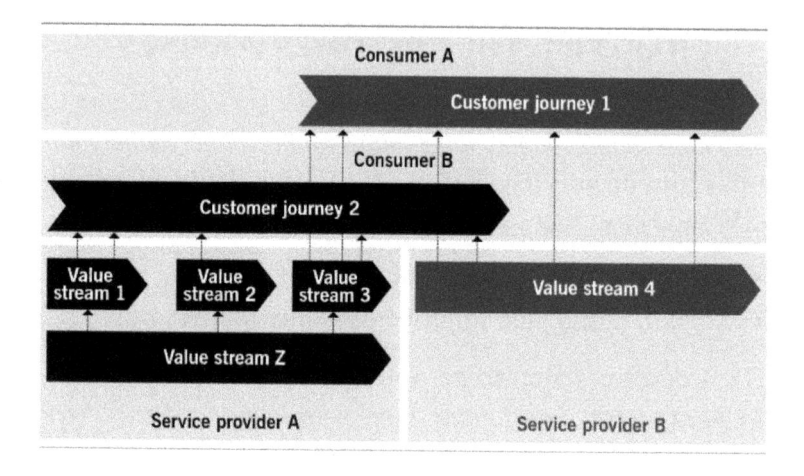

**Figure 1: Relationships between value streams and customer journeys**[1]

A customer journey will always rely on one or more value streams from one or more service providers. A customer journey can include multiple value streams from one service provider, or value streams from different service providers.

A value stream can support multiple customer journeys. The customer journey includes value stream activities that are part of what is known as the 'band of visibility'. There will be other value stream activities that are not visible to the customer, so these value streams don't form part of the customer journey.

The customer journey isn't always linear. It can involve moving around between different touchpoints, and repeated contact at some touchpoints. The customer might start in the

---

[1] *ITIL® 4: Drive Stakeholder Value*, figure 1.4. Copyright © AXELOS Limited 2020. Used under permission of AXELOS Limited. All rights reserved.

## 1: The customer journey

middle of the expected customer journey, so the service provider needs to continually monitor customer journeys and improve its understanding of customer behaviour.

> Think about your own customer journeys for the services you use every day. For example, a TV streaming service, or an insurance product. Where did your customer journey start? Has it finished? What value streams have supported your journey? You could think about new user onboarding, billing, customer service, etc. as examples of value streams.

Customer journeys are an important part of the overall customer and user experience. Customer experience (CX) is *"the sum of functional and emotional interactions with a service and service provider as perceived by a customer"*. User experience (UX) is *"the sum of the functional and emotional interactions with a service and service provider as perceived by a user"*.

The customer journey forms part of the customer's overall perception of a service provider, along with other influencing factors like brand, reputation, previous experiences, etc.

Figure 2 shows the three aspects of customer and user experience.

*1: The customer journey*

```
         Customer/user
         experience
Perceived                Perceived
brand                    service
touchpoints              environment

      Perceived customer/user journey
```

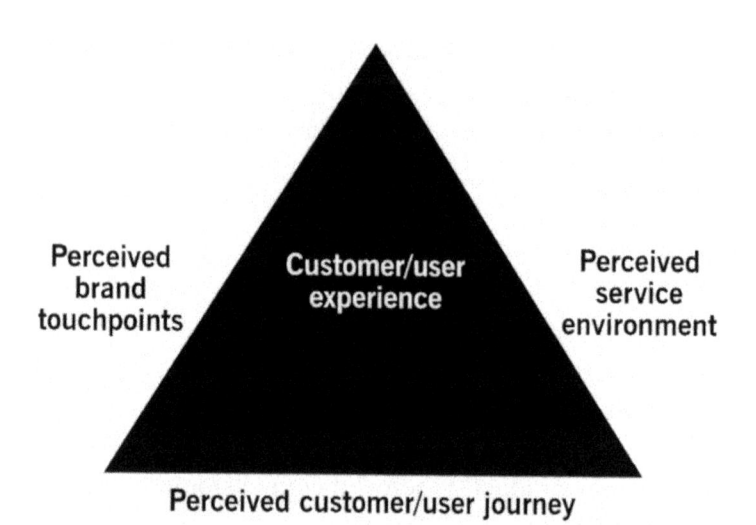

**Figure 2: Three aspects of the customer and user experience[2]**

The definitions for both customer and user experience mention 'emotional interactions'. This is an important point for you to consider as a service provider or in a service management role. In the past, we've not always considered the human element of service interactions. I've worked with organisations where there has been fierce resistance to change because the end users have an emotional attachment to a system they are using. It might not work very well, the new system might be a huge

---

[2] *ITIL® 4: Drive Stakeholder Value*, figure 1.5. Copyright © AXELOS Limited 2020. Used under permission of AXELOS Limited. All rights reserved.

*1: The customer journey*

> improvement, but I've seen a real sense of affection for older systems that can lead to a reluctance to change.
>
> As service providers, we can focus too much on the facts ("Why wouldn't you want this? It's twice as fast!") and miss the emotional elements. It's really important to have proper conversations with end users and customers so that we have the full picture and can carry out our role more effectively.

**Customer journey design**

Customer journey design is based on these principles:

- How you deliver a service is as important as what is delivered.
- The overall journey is more important than each individual touchpoint.
- Understanding the customer journey allows providers to focus on maximising value, and on experiences over outcomes.

The ITIL 4 Specialist: Drive Stakeholder Value syllabus and related publication are based around the steps in a customer journey.

These steps are:

- Explore
- Engage
- Offer
- Agree
- Onboard
- Co-create

*1: The customer journey*

- Realise

> Before you move on and learn about the customer journey in more detail, why not try creating your own customer journey map? You can use a product or service from your own organisation, or perhaps use Mortbank from the Banksbest case study. Note down what happens in each step of the customer journey, and refer back to it when we study the customer journey in more detail.

**Customer journey key concepts**

The key concepts related to a customer journey are:

- Benefits
- Stakeholder aspirations
- Journey mapping
- Personas
- Scenarios
- Maps
- Understanding the customer experience

We'll review them one by one in this section.

*1: The customer journey*

## *Benefits*

Understanding the customer journey delivers benefits for the service consumer and the service provider, as shown in table 1.

**Table 1: Customer Journey Mapping Benefits**

|  | **For the service consumer** | **For the service provider** |
|---|---|---|
| **Facilitate outcome** | Gain optimal service value and experience<br><br>Get what you need, not just what you asked for | Identify and support service consumer behaviours and outcomes<br><br>Optimise/improve products, services and journeys |
| **Optimise risk and comply** | Ensure key business risks are identified and addressed | Focus on customer satisfaction and maximise benefits for the investments |
| **Reduce cost and optimise resources** | Work together to optimise use of resources through the whole service lifecycle | Work together to optimise use of resources through the whole service lifecycle |

## *Stakeholder aspirations*

Stakeholders make choices based on their requirements. Value can be defined in the context of functional, social and

## 1: The customer journey

emotional dimensions. Service providers need to define the stakeholder experience aspiration, which is based on their needs, wants, stereotypes and emotions. Service choices are not always rational and logical, for example why would anyone pay more for a luxury hotel when a basic hotel option still delivers a bed in a room? What are the extra tangible and intangible service elements they are willing to pay for?

Defining the stakeholder experience aspiration allows the service provider to identify, understand and master the customer journey. Figure 3 shows the design steps.

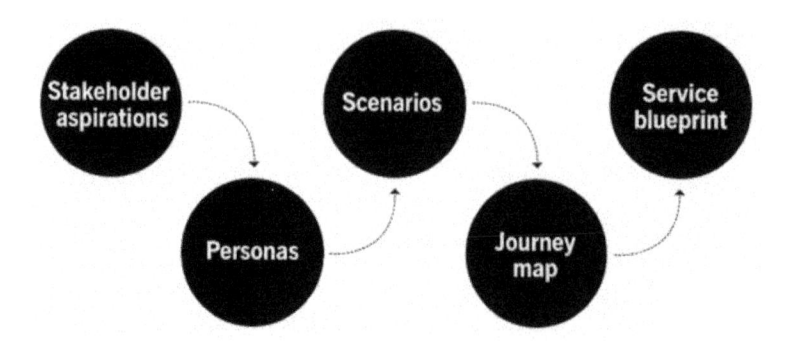

**Figure 3: The stages involved in designing end-to-end customer journeys and experiences[3]**

### *Journey mapping*

Customer journey mapping includes an understanding of touchpoints and service interactions.

---

[3] *ITIL® 4: Drive Stakeholder Value*, figure 2.2. Copyright © AXELOS Limited 2020. Used under permission of AXELOS Limited. All rights reserved.

# 1: The customer journey

*"A touchpoint is any event where a service consumer or potential service consumer has an encounter with the service provider and/or its products and resources."*

*"A service interaction is a reciprocal action between a service provider and a service consumer that co-creates value."*

Effective customer journey mapping optimises the whole journey; it is possible to have excellent touchpoints but a terrible overall experience. Customer journey maps need to take into account the mental models of the customer, and what level of service they expect.

A customer journey map helps an organisation understand its stakeholders. The journey map will include:

- Stakeholders;
- Time frame;
- Channels (e.g. social media, email, video, portals);
- Actions before the product or service experience;
- Actions during the product or service experience; and
- Actions after the product or service experience.

## *Personas*

*"A persona is a fictitious, yet realistic, description of a typical or target customer or user of a service or product."*

Creating personas can help support journey mapping exercises. It's not possible to map every single user journey, so personas are used to create generic flows. Personas are described as if they are real people, rather than being impersonal stereotypes.

## 1: The customer journey

> One of Banksbest's customer groups is residential landlords, who want mortgages for properties that they intend to rent out. Create a customer persona for a landlord, adding as much detail as you can based on your own experience and research. You could include a name, some personal and demographical information, their desired outcome, their motivations, what worries them, etc. You can also try this exercise for your own organisation's customers. How much do you know about them?

### *Scenarios*

Scenarios are *"short stories about personas trying to achieve their goals by using the service or product in their contexts"*. Service providers apply scenarios to customer segments and contexts.

Scenarios help the service provider to understand the ideal experience for each customer segment. These experiences can then be combined into a customer journey map that applies across segments.

A scenario will address these questions:

- Who is the user?
- Why does the service consumer want the service?
- What goals does the service consumer have?
- How can the service consumer achieve its goals?

*1: The customer journey*

I've had discussions with organisations about using tools and techniques including personas, scenarios, etc. Sometimes, I get feedback that "this will all take too long, why do we need to do it, things are going fine". The work required can seem daunting, but the benefits should not be underestimated. If you're starting this process in your own organisation, start small – for example, getting some key people together as a pilot to try to create a persona, or map a scenario. I often find an introductory session like this quickly highlights where assumptions are being made, or that there are gaps in organisational knowledge, and even where one team has a completely different perspective to another team. You can use these lessons to promote the effectiveness of these tools and techniques.

**Maps**

Figure 4[4] shows an example of a customer journey map.

---

[4] *ITIL® 4: Drive Stakeholder Value*, figure 2.3. Copyright © AXELOS Limited 2020. Used under permission of AXELOS Limited. All rights reserved.

*1: The customer journey*

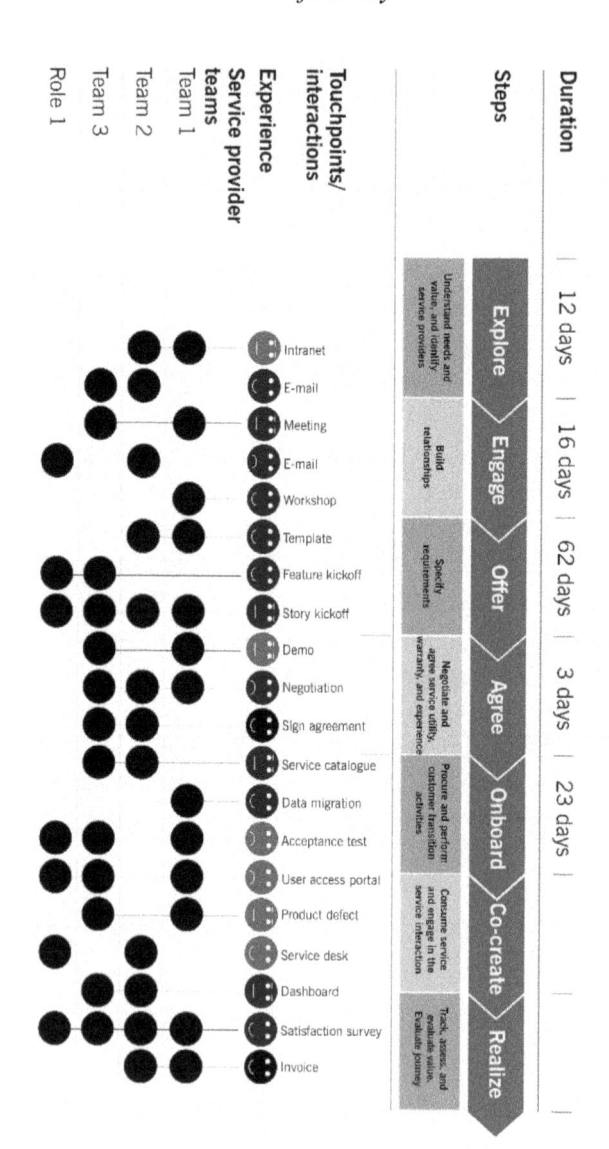

**Figure 4: Example of a customer journey map**

## 1: The customer journey

Simple customer journey maps will include:
- Steps
- Duration
- Touchpoints and interactions
- Personas
- Service experience
- Service provider teams and roles involved in customer interactions

### Understanding the customer experience

A customer's perception of services is shaped by many factors. Some of these factors can't be controlled by the service provider. To understand the customer experience, service providers need to look beyond the customer journey map, although it does provide a useful starting point.

Customer feedback surveys can help to provide valuable information. For example, consider asking questions like:

- What is the customer doing during a step in the customer journey?
- How do they feel?
- Are there any uncertainties that might stop them progressing through the journey?
- What cost and risk factors influence them?
- Do they have questions they can't find answers to?

Figure 5 shows the Johari Window, which can be used for service analysis.

*1: The customer journey*

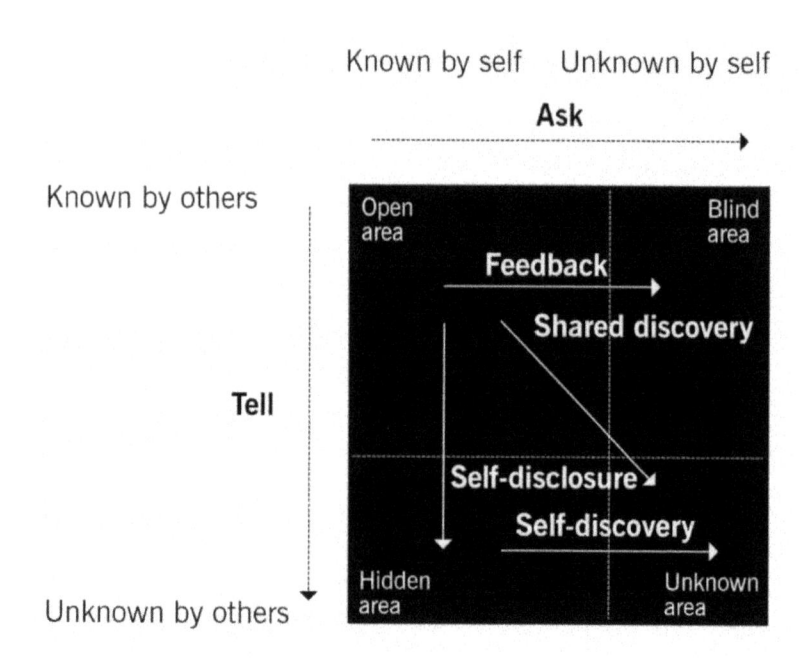

```
              Known by self    Unknown by self
                          Ask
       ┌─────────────────────────────────────►
       │  Open                    │    Blind
Known  │  area                    │    area
by     │         Feedback         │
others │        ──────────►       │
       │              Shared discovery
       │                   ╲      │
 Tell  │                    ╲     │
       │──────────────────────────│
       │              Self-disclosure ◤
       │                          │
       │              Self-discovery
       │             ──────────────►
       ▼  Hidden                  │   Unknown
          area                    │   area
Unknown by others
```

**Figure 5: The Johari Window**[5]

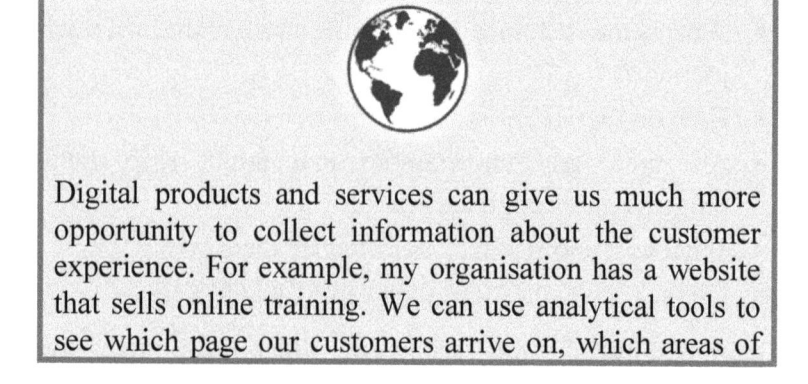

> Digital products and services can give us much more opportunity to collect information about the customer experience. For example, my organisation has a website that sells online training. We can use analytical tools to see which page our customers arrive on, which areas of

---

[5] *ITIL® 4: Drive Stakeholder Value*, figure 2.4. Copyright © AXELOS Limited 2020. Used under permission of AXELOS Limited. All rights reserved.

*1: The customer journey*

> the page they spend the most time interacting with and how far they get into the purchase journey. We can see where they drop out, how much time they spend on the site, and measure how many visits they make before going ahead with a purchase.
>
> We don't have a direct relationship with these customers because of the nature of interaction. We can't lean over their shoulders and talk to them and ask them what they are doing and why, but we can use the data we collect to understand their behaviour and try to improve our services accordingly. Once we make improvements, we can collect more data and check if we are getting the outcomes that we want.
>
> As service providers, we need to consider how we get the information we require to understand the customer experience. For my organisation, data is good, but we also need to find a way to have direct conversations and understand the emotional factors that are involved. As well as relying on what the technology can tell us, we need to speak to a sample of our customers and have a deeper conversation. Think about this in the context of your own organisation – how are you communicating with your customers?

**Designing and improving the customer journey**

As a service management practitioner, it's important to understand how to design and improve a customer journey, including:

- Design thinking;
- Leveraging behavioural psychology;
- Designing for different cultures; and

## 1: The customer journey

- Measuring and improving the customer journey.

Customer journeys need to be planned and designed to support optimal value co-creation and deliver the desired customer experiences. Customer journeys may include multiple products and services, and individual products and services may form part of multiple customer journeys. The customer journey can only be designed once the customer's desired outcome and customer and user experience have been defined.

### Design thinking

Design thinking puts the user at the centre of the design process. Designers need to engage with real users to be effective. One way to approach this is to use the 5 principles of design thinking. (Schneider and Stickdorn, 2012). The principles are shown in table 2.

**Table 2: 5 Principles of Design Thinking**

| | |
|---|---|
| **User-centred** | Customers and users are at the heart of the design process; real customers and users are consulted, without making assumptions based on data and averages. |
| **Co-creative** | Designs emerge from groups of stakeholders, including customers and users. The service provider isn't forcing a design onto its users, it is working co-creatively with them. |
| **Sequencing** | The customer journey is divided into touchpoints and service interactions. This allows the steps in the customer journey |

## 1: The customer journey

|  | to be analysed individually, from pre-service, through to service delivery, and to the post-service period. |
|---|---|
| Evidencing | Intangible services can be visualised as physical artefacts. These act as 'service evidence' that creates a response in the customer and builds an emotional association. |
| Holistic | The entire customer journey environment must be considered, including all the senses (hear, see, smell, touch, taste, feel). |

I'm sure that many of you reading this are feeling incredulous. Who doesn't do user-centred design? Why on earth would any service provider develop a product or service without speaking to the people who will use it? Sadly, my experience shows that many organisations still make mistakes here. They assume they know what their users want, or they think it will be too time-consuming to have proper conversations, or they fall in love with a piece of technology and create a solution that then needs to find a problem to solve.

The shift to Agile development is delivering real benefits. If an organisation is heading off down the wrong track, at

> least it will find out relatively early as it progresses through the iterative and incremental development process. A waterfall project could run for months or even years before potential problems are highlighted.

Customer journey design follows an iterative process, similar to product and service design.

**Table 3: Customer Journey Design**

| | |
|---|---|
| **Empathise** | Learn as much as possible about the stakeholders you are designing for, and their human needs. This includes building and testing personas and scenarios. Try to avoid assumptions as much as possible. |
| **Define** | This step builds a point of view based on user needs and the insights gained about them. This allows the definition of a plan for the desired outcome, experience and value. Goals and metrics can also be defined. |
| **Ideate** | In this step, brainstorming is used to identify creative solutions. This step gives the designers a variety of problem-solving ideas to work on, rather than a single perfect solution. |
| **Prototype** | A prototype could be an example customer journey map or service blueprint. The output should address frequency of activities, sequence and |

## 1: The customer journey

|  | |
|---|---|
|  | importance. The prototype helps to verify if the design helps deliver the planned outcome, experience and value. |
| **Test** | The original stakeholder group will provide feedback on the idea in this step. Testing should uncover errors or mistakes in the design, and can include usability testing, role-play and A/B testing. |

Customer journey design requires many skills, and can include product designers, graphic designers, interaction, social and ethnography designers, and more. Tools and techniques include stakeholder maps, storytelling, A/B testing, blueprints and the operating model canvas. These techniques are not examinable, but you may wish to do further research after your course if this is relevant for your career.

> The types of roles that are involved in customer journey design highlight one of the fundamental principles of digital transformation. Technology is now a core business capability, and isn't confined to the IT department. If our organisation relies on digital products and services, then all areas of the organisation could be involved in the design process. We need to stop thinking about 'IT and the business' as two completely separate domains.

## *1: The customer journey*

### *Leveraging behavioural psychology*

Humans are normally rational but can behave in irrational ways. Emotional intelligence and behavioural psychology can help designers build the emotional aspect of the customer journey. Cognitive biases, for example, affect customer behaviour. The table below shows some examples of different types of bias.

**Table 4: Types of Bias**

| | |
|---|---|
| **Peak-end bias** | This describes how consumers are more likely to remember 'peaks' of their service interaction, where the product or service experience was very positive or negative. You might have experienced this when reviewing input into customer satisfaction surveys; responses are often clustered around very high and very low satisfaction ratings. The customers who felt neutral about the interaction won't take the time to complete the survey. |
| **Availability bias** | The availability bias (or availability heuristic) describes how humans base judgements on events they can easily recall. For example, you might judge your Internet banking service by the one time it was unavailable, even though it had been consistently available for years before the outage. |
| **Loss aversion** | Humans are more concerned with losses than gains. This explains why some projects go on much longer than they |

## 1: The customer journey

> should; the project owners feel the loss of cancelling the project more intensely than is rational. You might have seen this referred to as the 'sunk cost fallacy' or 'throwing good money after bad'.

Understanding biases allows service providers to factor them into the design process. This might, for example, include:

- Providing consumers with choices to allow them to feel in control;
- Preventing 'surprises' that decrease satisfaction;
- Finishing the service interaction on a memorable, positive experience; and
- Moving any negative experiences to the start of the service interaction.

> Using the Banksbest case study, apply these principles to a business banking interaction. What choices could users be offered? What surprises need to be removed? What type of positive experience might be used to end the interaction?

*1: The customer journey*

### Designing for different cultures

A mental model is *"an explanation of someone's understanding of how something works in the surrounding world"*.

Culture is *"a set of values that is shared by a group of people, including expectations about how people should behave and their ideas, beliefs and practices"*.

Design needs to factor in mental models and cultural considerations. Cultural groups and personas include:

- Different countries
- Different industries
- Different teams in an organisation
- Different professions
- Different sectors (public, private, non-profit)

Culture maps can be used to support design. Two user groups are mapped to show similarities and differences in figure 6[6].

---

[6] *ITIL® 4: Drive Stakeholder Value*, figure 2.5. Copyright © AXELOS Limited 2020. Used under permission of AXELOS Limited. All rights reserved.

*1: The customer journey*

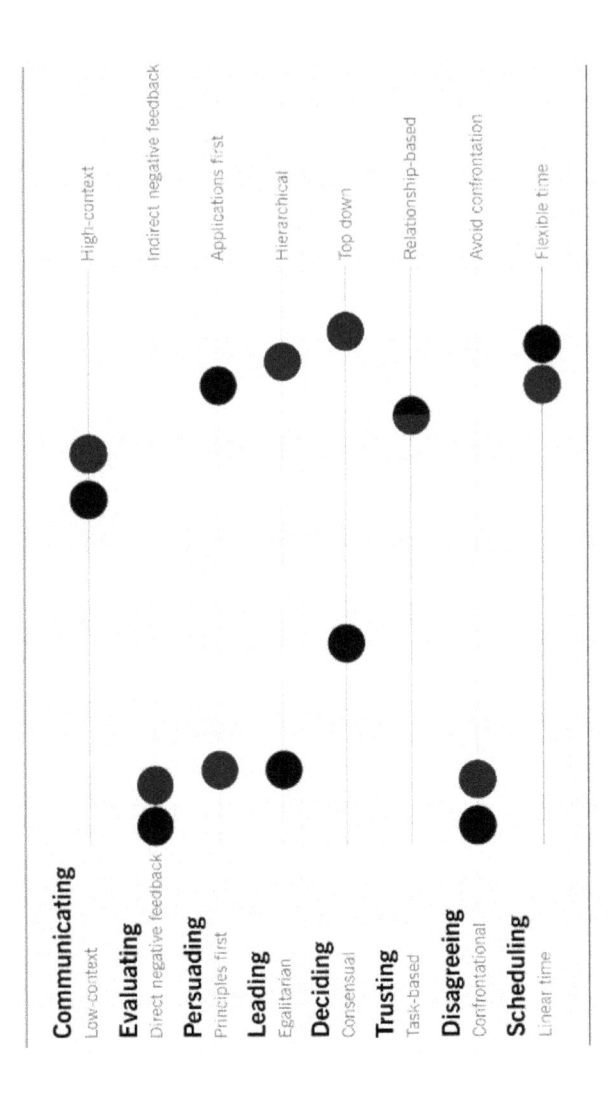

**Communicating**
Low-context — High-context

**Evaluating**
Direct negative feedback — Indirect negative feedback

**Persuading**
Principles first — Applications first

**Leading**
Egalitarian — Hierarchical

**Deciding**
Consensual — Top down

**Trusting**
Task-based — Relationship-based

**Disagreeing**
Confrontational — Avoid confrontation

**Scheduling**
Linear time — Flexible time

**Figure 6: The eight dimensions of culture**

## 1: The customer journey

### Measuring and improving the customer journey

Customer satisfaction isn't static. Service providers need to continually measure and improve feedback about the whole journey and the individual touchpoints and interactions. High-level customer experience metrics can be broken down into the customer journey, performance and outcome metrics to allow improvements to be identified. Improvement opportunities are prioritised, and problem management techniques can be applied to identify gaps and improvements.

---

At Banksbest, Lucy has three months before she will report back to the CDO and find out whether her project can continue. Feedback about the customer journey will be very important.

Consider the 'My Deposit My Way' feature that allows cheques to be paid in using a mobile phone camera. What are the advantages compared to the existing service, where the customer needs to use an ATM or visit a branch? What techniques could Lucy use to collect feedback about the new customer journey?

# CHAPTER 2: TARGETING MARKETS AND STAKEHOLDERS

This chapter is focused on step 1 of the customer journey: **explore**.

The topics include:

- The characteristics of markets;
- Marketing activities and techniques;
- How to describe customer needs;
- The internal and external factors that affect customer needs; and
- How to identify service providers and explain their value propositions.

Service providers need to understand their consumer's requirements to co-create value. When they do not have this understanding, they may make assumptions based on:

- Technology focus;
- Overconfidence;
- Acting before checking;
- Lack of time and resources; and
- Poor or no understanding of costs and risks.

## Understanding markets

A market contains sub-groups of service consumers and potential consumers. The consumers in a market have common characteristics that translate into similar product

## 2: Targeting markets and stakeholders

and service needs. Service providers will carry out market analysis to help them:

- Identify emerging opportunities and threats.
- Understand competitive advantage.
- Communicate with customers and markets.
- Allocate resources efficiently and effectively.

Market analysis is quantitative and qualitative and looks at market size and opportunities based on volume and value. This includes:

- *"Consumer segments*
- *Customer expectations and buying patterns*
- *Trends and dynamics*
- *Competition*
- *Key players*
- *Economic factors"*

**Market segmentation**

Service providers target market segments based on customer needs and expectations. Each market segment will be unique. Service providers can use market segments to understand how customers make decisions, allowing them to group customers and target products and services to them.

There are three factors that can help to identify market segments:

1. **Homogeneity** is a way of describing common needs;
2. **Distinction and uniqueness** show how the segment differs from others; and
3. **Reaction or response** to the market can also be studied.

## 2: Targeting markets and stakeholders

### *Characteristic-based market segmentation*

Figure 7 shows how characteristic-based market segmentation can be applied. Once characteristics are identified, the target group can be further analysed.

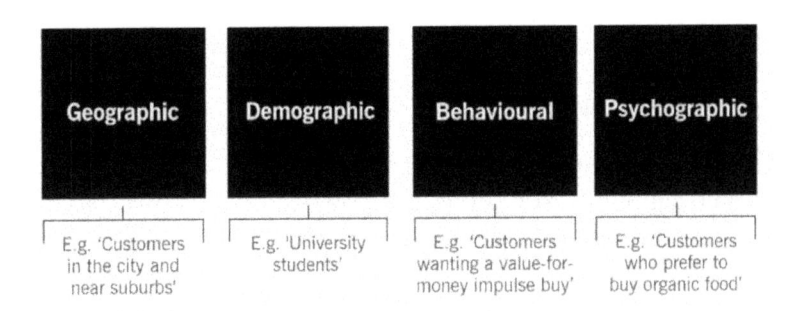

| Geographic | Demographic | Behavioural | Psychographic |
|---|---|---|---|
| E.g. 'Customers in the city and near suburbs' | E.g. 'University students' | E.g. 'Customers wanting a value-for-money impulse buy' | E.g. 'Customers who prefer to buy organic food' |

**Figure 7: Four bases for market segmentation[7]**

### *Needs-based market segmentation*

Needs-based market segmentation supports better communication with consumers. This process includes:

- Analysing existing consumers to identify where sales and demand originate;
- Exploring customer satisfaction and the drivers for purchasing decisions;
- Performing a SWOT* analysis;
- Categorising consumers; and
- Prioritising consumer segments.

---

[7] *ITIL® 4: Drive Stakeholder Value*, figure 3.3. Copyright © AXELOS Limited 2020. Used under permission of AXELOS Limited. All rights reserved.

## 2: Targeting markets and stakeholders

The service provider can then target their services and messaging in areas where they are most likely to be successful.

\* SWOT stands for Strengths, Weaknesses, Opportunities and Threats. Strengths and weaknesses are internal to a company. Opportunities and threats are external.

### Targeting markets

Marketing promotes products and services to consumers and market segments. Marketing is a profession in its own right; the areas that are relevant for us here are:

- Value propositions;
- Marketplace and marketspace;
- Personalising and profiling;
- Targeted marketing;
- Sustainability and the triple bottom line; and
- Existing customers.

### *Value propositions*

A value proposition is *"an explicit promise made by a service provider to its customers that it will deliver a particular bundle of benefits"*.

Value propositions should explain how the product or service solves problems, what consumers can expect, and why they should choose a particular organisation instead of its competitors.

## 2: Targeting markets and stakeholders

> **?**
>
> Banking is a challenging market to compete in, as many service providers are offering similar services and legislation and regulation can limit their ability to innovate. Think about some examples of value propositions that Lucy could use to help differentiate the Mibank service. What is being promised? Is there anything unique?

### *Marketplace and marketspace*

The marketplace is the physical world; a marketspace is defined by online channels.

Real-world marketing activities (marketplace) include:

- Seminars
- Sales meetings
- Conferences
- Printed advertising
- Networking events (face to face)

Online marketing activities (marketspace) include:

- Social media
- Articles
- Online advertising
- Websites
- Webinars and podcasts

- Blogs

The COVID-19 pandemic blurred the lines between marketplace and marketspace as typical 'real world' activities like conferences, face-to-face meetings and networking events shifted to cyberspace. Even the ability to use printed materials was affected due to hygiene concerns.

From the service management perspective, it was fascinating to watch how quickly technology evolved to meet the new requirements. In 2021, my organisation ran a virtual event for 300 people that included recorded content, live sessions, virtual networking tables, sponsor booths, etc. In fact, everything that you would expect from a live event (except for lunch). We received excellent feedback about how we had been able to create a 'community' feeling in a virtual space, but many delegates still expressed a desire to go back to face-to-face events as soon as possible.

Think about your own experiences and the changes in marketplace and marketspace since 2020. How do you think technology has adapted? Do you expect permanent behaviour changes from your customers, or do they see this as a temporary situation?

*2: Targeting markets and stakeholders*

## Personalising and profiling

Profiling tracks consumer behaviour to better understand their needs and support targeted marketing activities. For example, cookies on a website track which pages you visit, so that relevant products and adverts can be shown to you. Personalisation then targets specific content and offers to consumers. Organisations need to respect applicable legislation and obtain consent.

## Targeted marketing

Figure 8 shows the AIDA model, which expresses how personas are targeted using a staged 'funnel' approach. Service providers need to build complete funnels – awareness doesn't deliver any benefit if it doesn't convert into action.

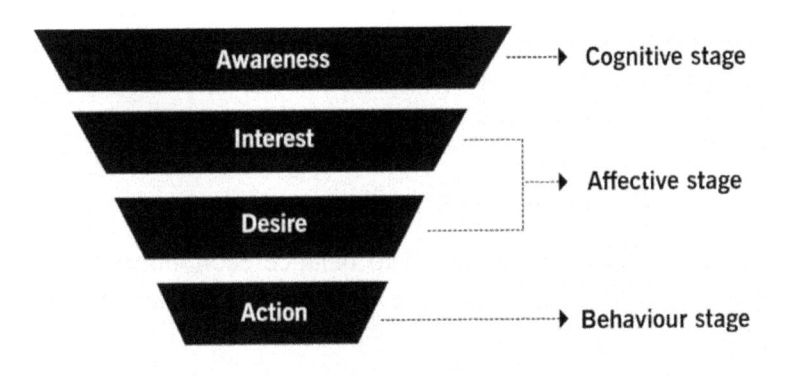

**Figure 8: The AIDA model**[8]

---

[8] *ITIL® 4: Drive Stakeholder Value*, figure 3.4. Copyright © AXELOS Limited 2020. Used under permission of AXELOS Limited. All rights reserved.

## 2: Targeting markets and stakeholders

### Brand and reputation

Brand defines how consumers perceive an organisation and its products and services. A service provider will try to create a strong brand, but ultimately the consumer decides how they respond to the brand. One-off events can affect an organisation's brand and reputation, in both positive and negative ways.

> Can you think of any events that have made you look at a brand in a new way? This could be something negative (for example, a data breach, or an ethical issue), or something positive (a brand that is supporting its community, or taking positive environmental action). Do these events affect your behaviour as a customer?

### Sustainability and the triple bottom line

Many organisations now seek to balance economic targets with sustainability goals. Figure 9 shows the sustainability and the triple bottom line approach.

## 2: Targeting markets and stakeholders

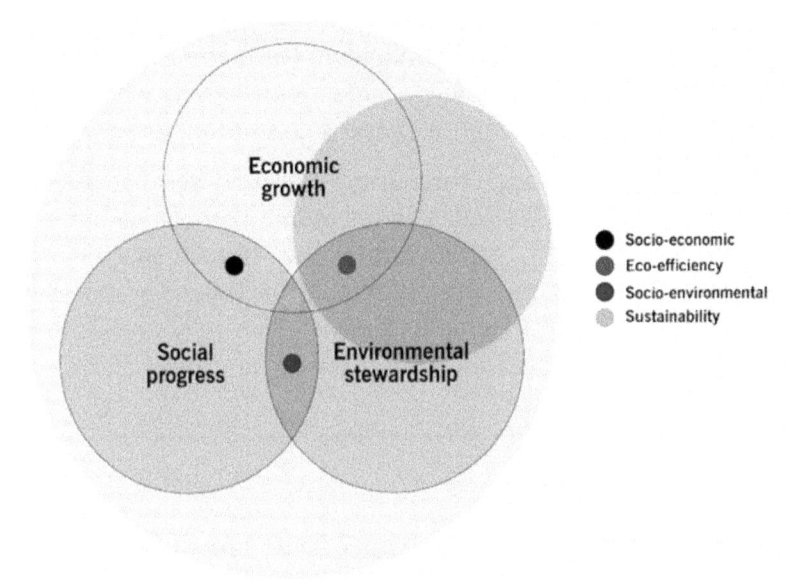

**Figure 9: Sustainability and the triple bottom line**[9]

Corporate social responsibility (CSR) has gained momentum in recent years as organisations try to demonstrate how they are contributing to society and the environment as well as meeting their financial goals. For organisations that take this seriously, there can be real benefits in terms of employee experience and morale,

---

[9] *ITIL® 4: Drive Stakeholder Value*, figure 3.5. Copyright © AXELOS Limited 2020. Used under permission of AXELOS Limited. All rights reserved.

## 2: Targeting markets and stakeholders

> better perception from shareholders (in fact, some funds only invest in ethical brands), and new customers who feel an emotional connection with the organisation.
>
> CSR initiatives without integrity, however, can backfire on an organisation. For example, some companies have been accused of 'greenwashing' or 'green sheen' – supplying misleading information to make their products seem more environmentally friendly than they are. This can have a negative impact on the organisation and its brand.

### *Existing customers*

Existing customers are an important source of repeat business and can also help to attract new customers, for example through 'word of mouth' marketing. Organisations nurture existing customers for these reasons:

- **Cost** – existing customers are cheaper to reach than new customers.
- **Resale** – existing customers may buy other products and services from the provider.
- **Brand** – they act as a 'marketing campaign' with word-of-mouth recommendations for products and services they are enjoying using.

Service providers should focus on building a strong relationship with consumers for the entire duration of their customer journey, not just on the single sale.

### Understanding customers and service providers

Service management practitioners need to be able to describe customer needs, and the internal and external factors that

## 2: Targeting markets and stakeholders

affect them. They also need to be able to identify service providers and their value proposition, including:

- External factors;
- Internal factors;
- SWOT analyses;
- Objectives and opportunities;
- Risks and mitigation;
- Identifying and analysing service consumers; and
- Understanding service providers and their offers.

A service consumer needs to be able to articulate its needs for a product or service. To do this, it must understand its purpose (as an individual or an organisation), and the internal and external factors that influence it. This understanding allows the consumer to make informed product and service decisions.

The 'golden circle', described by Simon Sinek, (figure 10) allows organisations to focus on their purpose.

*2: Targeting markets and stakeholders*

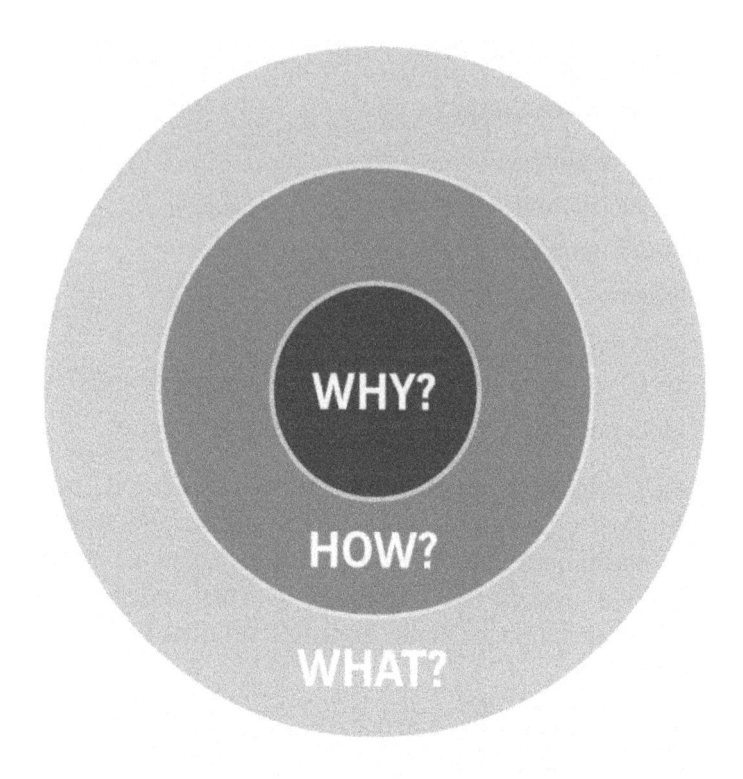

**Figure 10: The "golden circle"**[10]

A clearly defined organisational purpose motivates employees and helps to inform strategy and decisions. Stakeholder analysis of internal and external stakeholders helps to define how service value is created for the organisation.

---

[10] *ITIL® 4: Drive Stakeholder Value*, figure 3.1. Copyright © AXELOS Limited 2020. Used under permission of AXELOS Limited. All rights reserved.

## 2: Targeting markets and stakeholders

### *External factors*

A PESTLE analysis can be used to understand the external factors affecting an organisation. PESTLE tracks these areas:

- **Political:** For example, government policies, funding and grants, lobbying, corruption, bureaucracy.
- **Economic:** For example, taxation, seasonality, industry growth, international trade.
- **Sociological:** For example, culture, work ethic, media, consumer attitudes, ethical issues.
- **Technological:** For example, emerging technologies, research and development, innovation, intellectual property issues.
- **Legal:** For example, current and future legislation, employment law, regulatory bodies, tax regulations.
- **Environmental:** For example, geographic location, weather, energy supply.

---

Using the Bizbank service from the Banksbest case study, give an example of one factor for each area of PESTLE. For example, anti-money laundering regulations requiring the bank to collect proof of identity for each customer could be a legal factor. The PESTLE factors can be constraints during product and service development, but they can also highlight opportunities.

## 2: Targeting markets and stakeholders

### *Internal factors*

Internal factors provide a baseline of the organisation that can affect decisions to obtain or change services. The four dimensions of service management need to be assessed to provide a holistic view. Table 5 shows some of the areas and questions to address in an internal assessment.

**Table 5: Areas and Questions To Address In An Internal Assessment**[11]

| *Dimension* | *Areas to explore* | *Key questions* |
|---|---|---|
| *Value streams and processes* | *Key value streams* *Processes and services* *Current services* *Finance and profitability* | *Are the organization's purpose and objectives being supported?* *Where are the bottlenecks?* *Are the users happy with the current services?* |
| *Organizations and people* | *Organizational structure* *Roles and responsibilities* | *Are there efficient management structures?* |

---

[11] *ITIL® 4: Drive Stakeholder Value*, table 3.4. Copyright © AXELOS Limited 2020. Used under permission of AXELOS Limited. All rights reserved.

## 2: Targeting markets and stakeholders

| | | |
|---|---|---|
| | *Mapping of internal stakeholders* | *Are roles and responsibilities clearly defined?* |
| | *Organizational culture* | *Is there a service attitude?* |
| | *Internal skills and competencies* | *Do we have sufficient skills and competencies?* |
| | *Existing policies, processes and best practices* | *Is there information security awareness among employees?* |
| **Information and technology** | *Data and information* | *Does the information model match the business needs?* |
| | *Technology platform and architecture* | *Do we have proper technology and applications to support and digitize our services?* |
| | *Applications* | |
| | *Information security challenges* | *Are the right technical controls in place?* |

## 2: Targeting markets and stakeholders

| | | |
|---|---|---|
| **Partners and suppliers** | *Existing service providers, partners and suppliers*<br><br>*Contractual obligations* | *How well are the existing service providers being leveraged?*<br><br>*How well can the existing service providers fulfil our needs?* |

### SWOT analyses

A SWOT analysis can be used to combine internal and external assessment results. The following diagram shows a model of a SWOT analysis. The output from the analysis will then highlight areas where action is needed, for example an organisation with more weaknesses than strengths may need to obtain external services to boost its capabilities.

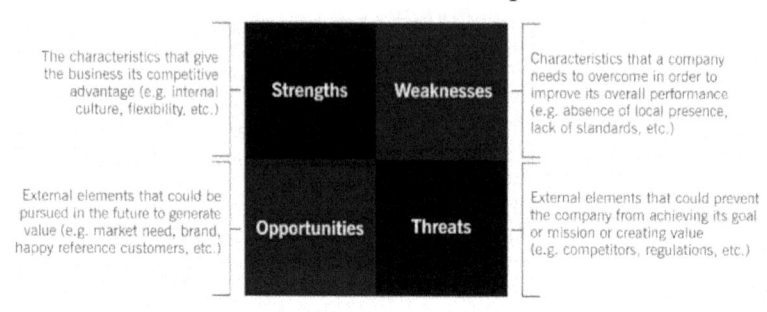

| | Strengths | Weaknesses | |
|---|---|---|---|
| The characteristics that give the business its competitive advantage (e.g. internal culture, flexibility, etc.) | | | Characteristics that a company needs to overcome in order to improve its overall performance (e.g. absence of local presence, lack of standards, etc.) |
| External elements that could be pursued in the future to generate value (e.g. market need, brand, happy reference customers, etc.) | Opportunities | Threats | External elements that could prevent the company from achieving its goal or mission or creating value (e.g. competitors, regulations, etc.) |

**Figure 11: Model SWOT Analysis**[12]

---

[12] *ITIL® 4: Drive Stakeholder Value*, figure 3.2. Copyright © AXELOS Limited 2020. Used under permission of AXELOS Limited. All rights reserved.

## 2: Targeting markets and stakeholders

### Objectives and opportunities

Once a consumer understands its needs, it can create service objectives and explore what is available. The ITIL 4 continual service improvement model shown in figure 12 provides an effective structure for these activities.

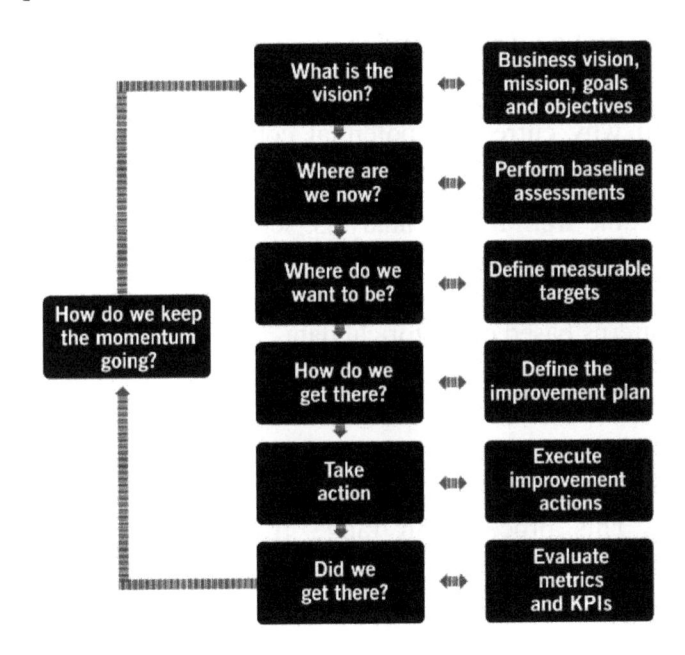

**Figure 12: The continual improvement model**[13]

### Risks and mitigation

During the explore step of the customer journey, risk assessment plays a key role. A risk profile will help to inform

---

[13] *ITIL® Foundation: ITIL 4 Edition*, figure 4.3. Copyright © AXELOS Limited 2019. Used under permission of AXELOS Limited. All rights reserved.

## 2: Targeting markets and stakeholders

decisions about the results, benefits, costs and opportunities that new or changed services will offer.

For example, decisions about whether to replace a legacy system with a new one, and whether to buy or build the new system, will be informed by the risk profile.

### Identifying and analysing service consumers

From the service provider's perspective, it is important to understand why current or potential consumers make the decisions they do about purchasing products or services.

Data can come from market analysis, segment analysis and analysis of small groups of consumers. Predictive analytics using technology such as machine learning can also help to predict patterns based on historical data.

### Understanding service providers and their offers

Once a consumer organisation understands what it needs, it must identify and evaluate potential services and service providers. This process can range from simple online research through to highly formal procurement and tender processes.

> The type of procurement process an organisation uses will be influenced by many different factors. The size of the organisation usually has an impact – small organisations will have relatively informal processes, and larger

## 2: Targeting markets and stakeholders

organisations will have much more formal processes with built-in checks and balances. Legislation and regulation also affect procurement processes, for example a public-sector organisation might be required to carry out steps to show it is using public money in a responsible way.

As with any process, it's very important to remember the first principle – procurement exists to help the organisation purchase services it needs. With my training business, we had one particularly frustrating experience where the customer department of an organisation wanted to work with us, but the procurement process was so restrictive it wasn't possible for us to become a supplier. The customer had to pay a premium to purchase our services via a reseller that was on the customer's preferred supplier list.

As with any activity in your organisation, procurement needs to be regularly reviewed to make sure it is still supporting overall business goals. Effective procurement practices should also protect an organisation from corrupt business dealings, so they are extremely important.

### *Industry standards and reference architectures*

Standards and architectures can affect service provider selection. These standards may be imposed by regulators or other bodies. The consumer needs to assess potential service providers for compliance with standards, including:

- *"Scope*
- *Principles*
- *Requirements*
- *Criteria*

## 2: Targeting markets and stakeholders

- *Classifications*
- *Controls*
- *Objects"*

# CHAPTER 3: FOSTERING STAKEHOLDER RELATIONSHIPS

This chapter is focused on step 2 of the customer journey: **engage**.

The topics include:

- Mutual readiness and maturity;
- Supplier and partner relationship types and their management;
- Developing customer relationships;
- Analysing customer needs;
- How the relationship management practice supports fostering relationships; and
- How the supplier management practice supports fostering relationships.

The engage step builds transparency, continual engagement and trust between stakeholders. Good relationships built on trust support value realisation. With high trust levels, customers increase demand and service providers can acquire resources to supply them, creating a virtuous cycle where both parties benefit.

Table 6 shows more information on the purpose of engaging and fostering relationships. Figure 13 shows the aspects of service value.

## 3: Fostering stakeholder relationships

**Table 6: The Purpose of Engaging and Fostering Relationships**[14]

| Engage | For the service consumer | For the service provider |
|---|---|---|
| Facilitate outcome and experience | To obtain higher (potential) value from services<br><br>To get better customer experience<br><br>To increase the effectiveness and efficiency of service design due to increased service provider buy-in<br><br>To reach a clearer shared understanding of expectations, needs, and preferences due to effective communication with the service provider | To increase service provisioning through nurturing and retaining existing customers<br><br>To strengthen competitive advantages in order to find and attract new customers<br><br>To gain improvement opportunities from better customer buy-in<br><br>To obtain better information for decision-making<br><br>To advance shared vision on how to achieve a win-win |

---

[14] *ITIL® 4: Drive Stakeholder Value*, table 4.1. Copyright © AXELOS Limited 2020. Used under permission of AXELOS Limited. All rights reserved.

## 3: Fostering stakeholder relationships

|  | To advance shared vision on how to achieve a win-win |  |
|---|---|---|
| Optimize risk and compliance | To reduce the level of complexity<br><br>To increase the probability of long-term success | To reduce the level of complexity<br><br>To increase probability of long-term success |
| Optimize resources and minimise cost | To reduce spending on services<br><br>To reduce spending on negotiations<br><br>To reduce time and effort to control activities | To reduce service costs<br><br>To reduce spending on negotiations<br><br>To reduce the cost of marketing and client service |

*3: Fostering stakeholder relationships*

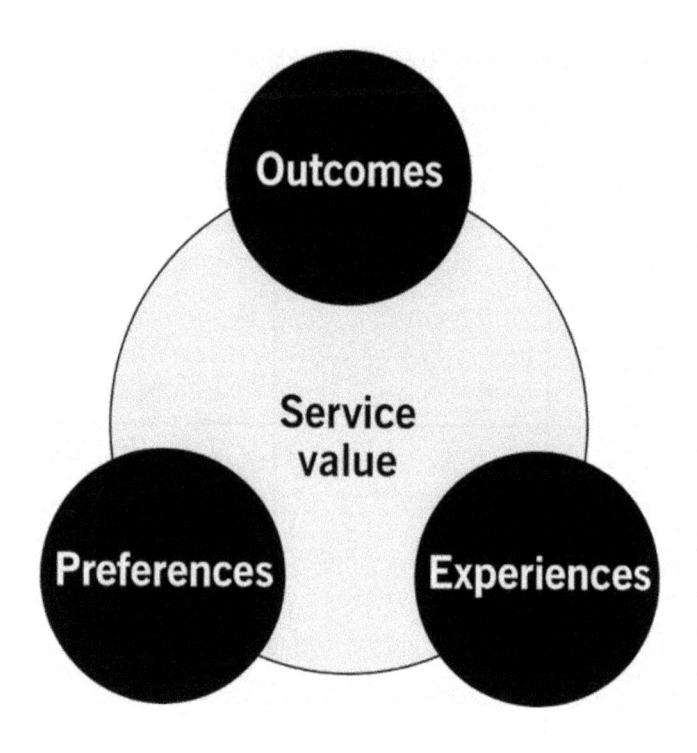

**Figure 13: Aspects of service value**[15]

## Supplier and partner relationships

### *Building service relationships*

Relationship management can be a role, a function, and/or a capability or practice in an organisation. Figure 14 shows the service relationship ladder, which is applied to the customer journey.

---

[15] *ITIL® 4: Drive Stakeholder Value*, figure 4.1. Copyright © AXELOS Limited 2020. Used under permission of AXELOS Limited. All rights reserved.

## 3: Fostering stakeholder relationships

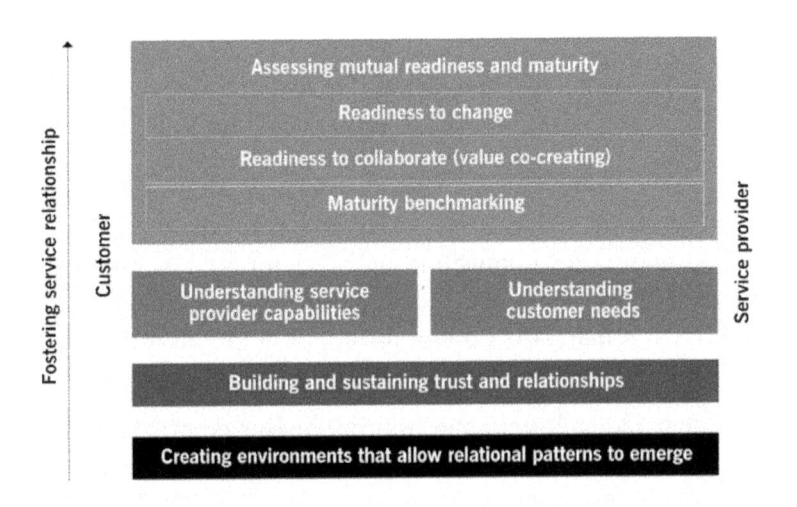

**Figure 14: The service relationship ladder**[16]

The Business Relationship Management Institute (BRMI)[17] defines three relationship metaphors:

- **Connector** – facilitates productive connections, shapes demand/supply, influences stakeholders.
- **Orchestrator** – orchestrates roles, resources, capabilities, coordinates and aggregates demand and supply.
- **Navigator** – facilitates convergence between stakeholders, facilitates planning, guides involved roles.

---

[16] *ITIL® 4: Drive Stakeholder Value*, figure 4.2. Copyright © AXELOS Limited 2020. Used under permission of AXELOS Limited. All rights reserved.

[17] Read more about the BRMI on its website: *https://brm.institute/*.

## 3: Fostering stakeholder relationships

> Think about the connector, orchestrator and navigator roles. Which one is the most important in your current position? What skills do you have that help you fulfil the role?
>
> Consider Doug Range and his role at Banksbest. Is he a connector, an orchestrator or a navigator? Does he fulfil more than one role?

Table 7 expands on the service relationship ladder concept.

**Table 7: The Steps of The Service Relationship Ladder**[18]

| Step | Description | ITIL management practices and tools |
|---|---|---|
| *Creating environments that allow relational patterns to emerge* | *Before any communication and collaboration starts, a service provider and a customer need to* | *Relationship management:*<br><br>*Managing communication channels* |

---

[18] *ITIL® 4: Drive Stakeholder Value*, table 4.7. Copyright © AXELOS Limited 2020. Used under permission of AXELOS Limited. All rights reserved.

## 3: Fostering stakeholder relationships

| Step | Description | ITIL management practices and tools |
|---|---|---|
| | have an encounter. The service provider should establish or take advantage of existing meeting places to bring the customer close enough to engage with and make mutual endeavours possible. | Providing points of contact<br><br>Marketing activities<br><br>Service catalogue management:<br><br>Use service catalogue as an invitation for the customer to begin conversation |
| Building and sustaining trust and relationship | After the customer has shown interest, building trust and relationship as the foundation of further value co-creation becomes crucial. | Relationship management (all activities and tools) |
| Understanding service provider | When the customer has chosen the | |

55

## 3: Fostering stakeholder relationships

| Step | Description | ITIL management practices and tools |
|---|---|---|
| capabilities (performed simultaneously with Step 4: Agree) | service provider, the customer wants to ensure that the service provider has a proper set of capabilities available, to fully leverage the provider capabilities. | |
| Understanding customer needs (performed simultaneously with Step 3: Offer) | Service relationship is mostly focused on satisfying service consumer needs. The service provider should leverage the relationship to uncover and understand the value that the customer wants to create. | Relationship management: Understanding customer needs activity Business analysis |

## 3: Fostering stakeholder relationships

| Step | Description | ITIL management practices and tools |
|---|---|---|
| *Assessing mutual readiness and maturity* | When the needs are understood, the final engagement questions on both sides can be answered. Service provider: are we capable of value co-creation with the customer? Do our resources and practices match customer needs? Customer: are we mature enough and ready to engage with the service provider, remembering all necessary constraints and activities needed in order to | *Business provider maturity model\** *Maturity assessment and audits* |

| Step | Description | ITIL management practices and tools |
|------|-------------|-------------------------------------|
|  | realise service value? |  |

*BRM Institute, 2014.

## Mutual readiness and maturity

Effective relationships rely on mutual readiness and maturity. This starts by mapping the context, including:

- Create an environment for the relationship to grow in;
- Build and sustain trust in the relationship;
- Understand service provider capabilities; and
- Understand customer needs.

Once the context is understood, service providers can assess the mutual level of readiness and maturity. If the service provider is immature, it might not be able to fulfil customer needs. If the customer or market is immature, it might not adopt a product or service.

## 3: Fostering stakeholder relationships

**Table 8: Types of Assessment In The Engage Step**[19]

|  | Basic relationship | Cooperative Relationship | Partnership |
|---|---|---|---|
| **Capabilities, maturity, and past performance (service provider)** | Crucial | Moderate | Minor |
| **Readiness to collaborate (both)** | N/A | Moderate | Crucial |
| **Readiness to change (customer)** | N/A | Moderate | Crucial |

### Supplier and partner relationships

There are many different types of service relationship. The ITIL 4 DSV publication focuses on three main archetypal service relationship types.

---

[19] *ITIL® 4: Drive Stakeholder Value*, table 4.14. Copyright © AXELOS Limited 2020. Used under permission of AXELOS Limited. All rights reserved.

## 3: Fostering stakeholder relationships

### Table 9: Service Relationship Types

|  | Basic relationship | Cooperative relationship | Partnership |
|---|---|---|---|
| **Relationship maturity** | Ad hoc, order taker. Reactive service without challenging customer requests, lack of quality data. | Service provider, (trusted) advisor. Both understand capabilities and needs. Mutual decision making, increasing sense of value. | Strategic partner. Common goals with focus on value. Clear accountability for achieving value, quality data for understanding value. |
| **Approach for building the relationship** | Frequent misperceptions and distrust. Reactive course changes, value may be hidden. | Routine is good but innovation is challenging. Portfolio aligned to business needs. Sense of value. | Shared goals for maximising value. Shared risk and reward. |
| **Key attributes** | Little information sharing. Price driven, easy to exit. Single point of contact. | Seek to add value. Many points of contact, expensive, forecasting, but not joint planning. | Deep trust and partnership. Acknowledge mutual importance. Free exchange of information. Hard to exit. |

## 3: Fostering stakeholder relationships

The level of trust and the amount of management required to maintain a supplier relationship will change over time. A change of personnel, a service disruption or a change to the consumer's business model can all affect the relationship. The following tables show some of the pros and cons of basic, cooperative and partnership relationships.

**Table 10: Pros and Cons of Relationship Types[20]**

| Basic Relationship | Advantages | Disadvantages |
|---|---|---|
| Service consumer | Easy to exit<br>Easy to control | Emphasis is placed on efficiency and transactions<br>Hard to develop a deeper relationship<br>Hard to assess service value |
| Service provider | Single channel of communication<br>Easy to measure and report<br>Building scale and operational efficiencies into | Emphasis is placed on efficiency and transactions<br>Difficult to develop a trustworthy relationship<br>Little to no information sharing |

---

[20] *ITIL® 4: Drive Stakeholder Value*, table 4.4. Copyright © AXELOS Limited 2020. Used under permission of AXELOS Limited. All rights reserved.

## 3: Fostering stakeholder relationships

| | service management practices Standard customer management approach | Easy for the customer to exit<br>Customer is driven by price<br>Little opportunity to deliver differentiated customer experiences |
|---|---|---|

**Table 11: Pros and Cons of Relationship Types[21]**

| Cooperative Relationship | Advantages | Disadvantages |
|---|---|---|
| Service consumer | The service provider tailors the service to specific service consumer needs<br><br>New opportunities to do more business with the service provider | Mutual activities may feel uncoordinated<br><br>Expensive and resource-intensive |
| Service provider | Higher service consumer dependency on | Mutual activities may feel uncoordinated |

---

[21] *ITIL® 4: Drive Stakeholder Value*, table 4.5. Copyright © AXELOS Limited 2020. Used under permission of AXELOS Limited. All rights reserved.

## 3: Fostering stakeholder relationships

| | | |
|---|---|---|
| | the service provider | Expensive and resource-intensive |
| | More information is received from the customer; opportunity to be far more effective in helping to drive valuable solutions | Higher risk of mistakenly allocated resources |
| | | New operational complexities emerge |
| | | Customer brings internal problems to the service provider |
| | | Less efficiency and control over customers |

**Table 12: Pros and Cons of Relationship Types[22]**

| Strategic Relationship | Advantages | Disadvantages |
|---|---|---|
| Service consumer | Transparency allows both sides to identify inefficiencies and work together to fix them, which leads to mutual cost reductions | Lock-in may prevent the customer from increasing requirements or exiting |
| | Long-term planning opens new market opportunities | Separation is painful and time-consuming |

---

[22] *ITIL® 4: Drive Stakeholder Value*, table 4.6. Copyright © AXELOS Limited 2020. Used under permission of AXELOS Limited. All rights reserved.

## 3: Fostering stakeholder relationships

| Service provider | Transparency allows both sides to identify inefficiencies and work together to fix them, which leads to mutual cost reductions<br><br>Long-term planning opens new market opportunities<br><br>Chance to attract bigger and more strategic customers | Separation is painful and time-consuming |

> The level of trust that you feel for a supplier or partner will evolve over time. Normally, a long relationship allows events to be viewed in perspective. A negative event such as a major incident can be catastrophic for a new supplier relationship, and less so for a long-established relationship. The *SIAM Professional Body of Knowledge*[23] provides examples of events that can affect the level of trust in a relationship, including:

---

[23] For more information, visit:
*www.itgovernancepublishing.co.uk/product/service-integration-and-management-siam-professional-body-of-knowledge-bok-second-edition*.

## 3: Fostering stakeholder relationships

> - At the start of a relationship, when the supplier has not proven they can deliver the service;
> - When a supplier over-promises and then cannot deliver;
> - When key personnel change; and
> - When the customer puts too much pressure on the supplier, beyond contractual obligations.
>
> If your role involves working with key suppliers, it's important to have strategies in place to build and maintain strong relationships. In former roles I have used many different techniques, from social events to regular service reviews. The strategies that work best for you will depend on many factors including the business culture you work within, any historical relationship, and the willingness of your suppliers to engage. When a crisis hits and you need your suppliers to go above and beyond, the time you spend investing in strong relationships will be fully repaid.

Increasingly, service providers are used as 'service hubs', which coordinate suppliers and partners on the customer's behalf. They may act as a 'black box', where the details of sub-contractors are invisible to the customer. This change in demand has led to the development of **service integration and management** (SIAM™[24]).

There are four main service integration models defined in ITIL 4:

---

[24] Learn more about SIAM at *www.scopism.com*. SIAM™ is a registered trademark of EXIN.

## 3: Fostering stakeholder relationships

- **Retained organisation** – the retained organisation (the customer organisation) manages vendors and coordinates SIAM itself.
- **Single supplier** – a vendor provides all services plus the SIAM function.
- **Service guardian** – a vendor provides the SIAM function plus one or more delivery functions.
- **Separate service integrator** – a vendor provides the SIAM function but doesn't deliver any other services.

## Customer relationships

### Developing customer relationships

The service provider will guide their customer through four stages, outlined in the table below.

**Table 13: Developing Customer Relationships**

| | |
|---|---|
| **Awareness** | The customer should be aware of the service and/or provider. The customer is carrying out market research, so the service provider will need to reach them through its network and its marketing. |
| **Motivation** | The customer wants to start a relationship with the service provider, which will help them understand what is available and stimulate demand from them. |
| **Contacting** | The customer needs to understand how to contact the service provider and what is offered, perhaps by looking at a service |

## 3: Fostering stakeholder relationships

|  | catalogue. The service provider needs to make this information clear and relevant. |
|---|---|
| **Shaping expectations** | The customer will expect a good experience, and the service provider will support this by making information and references available to support research by the customer and will make sure it has the right resources to provide the service. |

The initial engagement between consumer and service provider is supported by the service catalogue. The service catalogue provides information about services and performance, and may include financial data. The service provider will give more detailed information to the consumer if required. The service provider may also provide access to service information via a customer relationship management (CRM) system.

The service provider's goal is to create an environment where relational patterns* can develop. The service provider needs to actively manage this, considering that:

- Irregular communication will have a negative impact on any relationship;
- Points of contact who don't respond promptly also create bad feeling;
- Service incidents can lead to conflict that needs to be managed; and
- Risk management can help develop an approach to disturbances in the service provider, the customer organisation or the market overall.

## 3: Fostering stakeholder relationships

* Relational patterns "are the repeated and consistent ways in which we interact with and respond to people with whom we are in a relationship. This includes any and all relationships – from parent to spouse, to friend or client".[25] These patterns develop in a manner much like that of language acquisition.

> Using the Banksbest case study, think about the Mortbank service. A customer might use the service for decades as they pay down their mortgage, but they will not necessarily expect regular communication. How should Banksbest interact with these customers? What patterns will emerge? For example, consider an annual statement, or a regular review with a mortgage manager. What benefits would this type of interaction create?

***Building and sustaining trust***

The service provider and the customer must work together to create value, in a relationship underpinned by trust. The ITIL 4 relationship management practice addresses internal relationships (business relationship management, or BRM) and external relationships (customer relationship

---

[25] Source: *https://womenbelong.com/relational-patterns-why-they-matterfor-everyone/*.

*3: Fostering stakeholder relationships*

management, or CRM). Trust will develop and levels of trust will change over time.

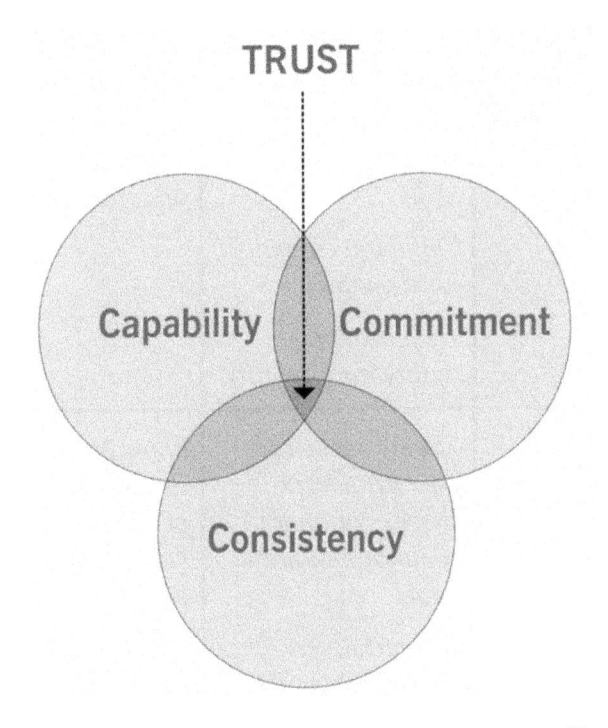

**Figure 15: Three Cs trustworthiness model**[26]

Tables 14 and 15 provide further detail about the three Cs model.

---

[26] *ITIL® 4: Drive Stakeholder Value*, figure 4.3. Copyright © AXELOS Limited 2020. Used under permission of AXELOS Limited. All rights reserved.

## 3: Fostering stakeholder relationships

**Table 14: The Three Cs Model Applied To A Service Relationship**[27]

| Trust factor | Service provider | Customer |
|---|---|---|
| Capability | Adequate knowledge and skills<br><br>Sufficient capacity for demand<br><br>Demonstrate agility/adaptability | Demonstrate agility/adaptability |
| Commitment | Show concern for the customer's success or share common/mutual goals<br><br>Be honest, respectful, and cooperative<br><br>Explain actions that impact the customer<br><br>Be familiar with the service | Show concern for the service provider's success or share common/mutual goals<br><br>Be honest, respectful, and cooperative<br><br>Explain changes that impact the service provider<br><br>Encourage/ |

---

[27] *ITIL® 4: Drive Stakeholder Value*, table 4.9. Copyright © AXELOS Limited 2020. Used under permission of AXELOS Limited. All rights reserved.

## 3: Fostering stakeholder relationships

|  | consumer and its needs | promote open, two-way communication |
|---|---|---|
|  | Encourage/ promote open, two-way communication |  |
| **Consistency** | Seek first to understand, then to be understood | Seek first to understand, then to be understood |
|  | Deliver expected performance over time | Disclose adequate amount of information |
|  | Respond in a timely manner |  |

**Table 15: Relationship Management Service Integrator Activities[28]**

| *Step* | *Service integrator activities* |
|---|---|
| **Creating environments that allow relational patterns to emerge** | *Scan the consumer landscape in search for new suppliers and partners that may enable realization of the consumer strategy and objectives* |

---

[28] *ITIL® 4: Drive Stakeholder Value*, table 4.19. Copyright © AXELOS Limited 2020. Used under permission of AXELOS Limited. All rights reserved.

## 3: Fostering stakeholder relationships

|  |  |
|---|---|
|  | Contact and negotiate with possible suppliers<br><br>Check the past performance and/or public ratings of suppliers and manage due diligence (if relevant) |
| **Building and sustaining trust and relationships** | The same as for a normal service relationship |
| **Understanding service provider capabilities** | Define criteria for managing suppliers based on relationship type, level of dependency, and risk<br><br>Identify and categorize existing suppliers according to criteria and focus on the most important suppliers<br><br>Assess suppliers' capabilities according to the needs of the customer |
| **Understanding service consumer needs** | The same as for a normal service relationship |
| **Assessing mutual readiness and maturity** | Track suppliers' performance and compliance<br><br>Assess suppliers' maturity<br><br>Assess the larger supply chain and manage risk related to the suppliers |

## 3: Fostering stakeholder relationships

|  | *and their subcontractors influencing suppliers' ability to deliver services* |

> **?**
>
> In the Banksbest case study, you have seen that MortSys, the developer of the Mortbank service, doesn't always respond within the target times for its services. We can assume that this creates tension in the relationship. What can Banksbest and Mortbank do to improve this?

Different relationship types require different relationship management activities. For example, a basic relationship requires a customer to share requirements with the service provider, but a partnership requires more than that; the two parties must create an open platform for collaboration. Table 16 provides more detail about relationship management activities for each relationship type.

## 3: Fostering stakeholder relationships

**Table 16: Relationship Management Activities**[29]

| Relationship type | Building trust and relationship approach | Customer | Service provider |
|---|---|---|---|
| Basic relationship | Trust and relationships are built primarily through following formal procedures and controls | Share requirements with the service provider<br><br>Check past performance of service provider<br><br>Check public ratings and feedback from past and current customers<br><br>Due diligence/ check evidence of compliance with industry standards and/or certifications | Manage service catalogue and service requests catalogue<br><br>Do not challenge requests from the customer<br><br>Satisfy demand/ limit collaboration to the scope of the service catalogue<br><br>Provide reports<br><br>Focus on outputs |

[29] *ITIL® 4: Drive Stakeholder Value*, table 4.10. Copyright © AXELOS Limited 2020. Used under permission of AXELOS Limited. All rights reserved.

## 3: Fostering stakeholder relationships

| Relationship type | Building trust and relationship approach | Customer | Service provider |
|---|---|---|---|
| | | Check SLA | |
| Cooperative relationship | Trust and relationships are built primarily through extensive communication and efforts of each party, made in order to achieve outcomes<br><br>Aligned outcomes, feedback, semi-formal controls | Share needs<br><br>Be open to service provider's proposals<br><br>Perform audit or maturity assessment cross references | Manage and develop service portfolio according to changing customer needs<br><br>Advise on possible service solutions<br><br>Be driven by outcomes, not outputs |
| Partnership | Trust and relationships are built primarily through sharing risks and rewards and focus on | Establish open platforms for collaboration with the service provider | Establish open platforms for collaboration with the customer<br><br>Demonstrate capability to enable |

## 3: Fostering stakeholder relationships

| Relationship type | Building trust and relationship approach | Customer | Service provider |
|---|---|---|---|
| | shared goals and value co-creation | Share goals, risks, and rewards<br><br>Joint strategic/program/projects planning<br><br>Demonstrate agility and adaptability to the changing environment | consumer development and innovation<br><br>Focus on value realization in changing environment, not on fixed outcomes |

### Continually building trust

Many factors affect trust and relationships, including:

- Separation between service provider and service consumer organisations;
- Change in personnel or resources;
- Customer complaints; and
- Misaligned goals and objectives.

The service provider and the service consumer need to work together to continually improve their relationship.

## 3: Fostering stakeholder relationships

> Think about a service provider you have an ongoing relationship with. It could be a bank, an insurance company, an online shop, etc.
>
> How do you rate your relationship with the organisation? What does it do that strengthens the relationship? Is there anything it has done that weakened the relationship? Is there anything required from you to improve the relationship?

### *Understanding service provider capabilities*

Audits and maturity assessments can be used to understand service provider capabilities. This can be done using externally available information such as references, or in collaboration with the service provider and assessing the details of their processes and procedures.

Any assessment should cover the four dimensions of service management. If a service provider does not have the right capabilities, it may not be able to deliver the required service, and this will be a poor foundation for any future relationship.

**Analysing customer needs**

### *Communication and collaboration*

Communication is an essential part of relationship building. During the engage step, communication is part of the initial expectation setting for the service consumer. Poor

## 3: Fostering stakeholder relationships

communication can lead to delays, unnecessary costs and disputes, and poor service delivery.

Cooperation and collaboration are both effective and valuable approaches to teamwork, both within and across organisations. In service relationships, cooperation is common in basic and cooperative relationships; at the partnership level, both parties need to work towards collaboration. To communicate and collaborate effectively, consider cultural differences, language barriers and time zones.

ITIL 4 defines cooperation as *"... working with others to achieve your own goals"* and collaboration as *"... the process whereby a person or persons work with one another to produce something"*.

Listening is an essential part of communication. It can be improved by practice and training. Stephen Covey's scale of listening includes:

- **Ignoring** – no effort;
- **Pretending** – the appearance of listening;
- **Selective listening** – hearing what you want to hear;
- **Attentive listening** – focusing on the speaker; and
- **Empathetic listening** – listening and responding to the speaker's words, intent and feelings.

There are three modes of listening that you might have experienced in service management or personal situations.

## 3: Fostering stakeholder relationships

Table 17: Modes of Listening[30]

| | |
|---|---|
| **Internal Listening** | *"Description: Focus is inward. Most of the attention is given to how the subject affects the listener, what emotions it invokes, and how it compares with individual preconceptions.*<br><br>*When to use: This type of listening is useful when participating as the user in training, or reviewing work results reports, learning new instructions, being coached or mentored, reviewing documentation, etc.*<br><br>*Covey's scale: Ignoring, pretend listening, selective listening"* |
| **Focused Listening** | *"Description: Focus is on the other person, not much attention is paid to the outside world. Focused listening is a level of empathy, clarification, and collaboration. Listeners notice tone, body language, and ongoing reactions throughout the conversation.*<br><br>*When to use: This type of listening may be used when discussing requirements for a service (e.g. negotiating SLAs), participating in decision making meetings, planning changes etc.* |

---

[30] Based on *ITIL® 4: Drive Stakeholder Value*, table 4.2. Copyright © AXELOS Limited 2020. Used under permission of AXELOS Limited. All rights reserved.

## 3: Fostering stakeholder relationships

|  | *Covey's scale: Attentive listening"* |
|---|---|
| **Global Listening** | *"Description: Global listening, or environmental listening, includes everything that can be observed through all senses. Good performers usually have strong global listening skills. Experienced actors, trainers, teachers, and leaders may have been able to instantly assess an atmosphere and monitor how it changes in response to their actions. These people are good at adjusting their behavior according to the impact they make.*<br><br>*When to use: This type of listening may be used when solving problems, when designing products and services, in teaching, when conducting audits, when coordinating teamwork, and in sales situations. The service provider communicates with the service consumer through surveys, social media, customer reviews, emails, feedback forms, service usage analytics, etc.*<br><br>*Covey's scale: Empathetic listening"* |

Service relationships in today's environment can be affected by cultural and language differences, time zones, seasonal factors and organisational culture.

To foster relationships, one must:

- Be respectful;
- Use the 'right' language (which can change over time);

## 3: Fostering stakeholder relationships

- Create a psychologically safe environment;
- Be clear, and create actionable statements; and
- Continually check messages are received and understood.

Have you ever kept quiet because you didn't want to look stupid? Maybe you didn't ask a question on a training course because everyone else seemed to understand the concept, or you didn't mention something looked risky because you didn't want to get into trouble. Most of us have been in this situation, and our behaviour is often shaped by the environment that we're in. If we work for a manager who mocks people who ask questions, we learn very quickly to keep quiet.

The opposite of this is a 'psychologically safe environment'. Psychological safety is defined by Amy Edmondson from Harvard Business School as "a belief that one will not be punished or humiliated for speaking up with ideas, questions, concerns or mistakes".

In an environment where people feel safe asking questions, or trying new things, you will find strong teams. People feel comfortable sharing ideas and are more likely to experiment, leading to more innovative products and services.

Think about the culture in your organisation and how safe it feels. If it's not a safe environment, what can you do to

> change that? If this is a relevant topic for you, I recommend watching professor Amy Edmondson's TEDTalk on "Building a psychologically safe workplace".

## Understanding customer needs

Customers don't buy services; they buy fulfilment of needs. So, how do we understand what our customers need? How do we know what job the customer is trying to do? This can be even more challenging when technical solutions are involved, as the customer may not be able to clearly articulate their needs. There needs to be an ongoing dialogue between service provider and consumer.

## Value drivers

Customers want outcomes. The BRM Professional publication from the BRMI outlines two approaches to link outcomes to products and services:

- **Value-based (top down)** – the service provider discovers the customer's most urgent problems or objectives, and then analyses initiatives and technology to address them.
- **Solution-based (bottom up)** – the service provider reviews its products and services and looks at how to connect them to customer problems and objectives.

To help understand customer needs, ask questions such as:

- What are the major issues?
- What are the causes of these issues?

## 3: Fostering stakeholder relationships

- How do these issues affect the consumer's purpose, objectives and performance?
- What is the current service consumer context?

Risks and costs need to be analysed as part of customer needs analysis. Some costs and risks will be removed by a service, and others will be introduced. Experiences and preferences are also relevant; preferences will have an influence on the service consumer, particularly in business-to-consumer (B2C) sales where the consumer is an individual.

**The relationship management practice**

The purpose of the relationship management practice is *"to establish and nurture the links between the organization and its stakeholders at strategic and tactical levels"*.

To achieve this purpose, the relationship management practice establishes a culturally based, consistent approach for interaction with its stakeholders (e.g. users, customers, partners, suppliers, and others).

The cultural basis includes aspects such as:

- *"Shared or mutually recognized goals*
- *No-blame cooperation and collaboration*
- *Continuous learning*
- *Open and transparent communications*
- *Conflict prevention and mediation"*

Stakeholder management is critical to relationship management. To be successful, think broadly to identify the internal and external stakeholders.

Any interaction in a relationship is between people. The impact of human nature and values should be remembered as

## 3: Fostering stakeholder relationships

each relationship is managed. Understanding the organisational cultural differences, including the type of relationship (commercial/non-commercial), level of formality, group or individual dynamics, level of professionalism, as well as the perceived hierarchy between the parties, will enhance the relationship.

> At Banksbest, Lucy is the product owner for the My Way project. Who are her stakeholders? List as many as you can think of, based on the case study and the assumptions you can make based on your own experience.
>
> What about your role? Which stakeholders do you have? How much time do you spend managing stakeholder relationships?

### *Practice success factors (PSFs)*

There are three practice success factors for relationship management:

- *"Establish and continually improve an effective and healthy approach to relationship management across the organization*
- *Ensure effective and healthy relationships within the organization*
- *Ensure effective and healthy relationships between the organization and its external stakeholders"*

## 3: Fostering stakeholder relationships

**Table 18: PSF: Establish and Continually Improve The Relationship Management Approach**

| PSF: Establish and continually improve the relationship management approach |
|---|
| How relationships are handled in an organisation will reflect organisational values, such as openness, collaboration, no-blame and psychological safety. |
| Working with other practices, such as workforce and talent management, strategy management and supplier management, the relationship management practice will develop and maintain techniques that reflect these values. How relationships are managed is strongly related to the organisational strategy as well as how external factors (PESTLE) impact the organisation. Ensure that any behaviour rules are adopted and followed across the organisation. |

**Table 19: PSF: Ensure Effective and Healthy Internal Relationships**

| PSF: Ensure effective and healthy internal relationships |
|---|
| To create effective external relationships, a strong internal culture must exist. We know how important customer or user satisfaction is to the success of an organisation. Employee satisfaction is just as important. |
| Organisations have focused on protecting previously vulnerable groups (e.g. embracing diversity) and made greater efforts to understand and foster job and employee |

## 3: Fostering stakeholder relationships

> satisfaction. Ensure a formal assessment of internal environmental conditions occurs when there is a change in the organisational environment (new strategy, change in organisational structure, etc.).
>
> Understand the organisational climate – it will be reflected in the relationships the organisation develops. Happy employees lead to happy users and customers.

**Table 20: PSF: Ensure Effective and Healthy External Relationships**

| PSF: Ensure effective and healthy external relationships |
|---|
| External relationships include customers, users and sponsors. The key measurement for these service relationships is simple: customer satisfaction. Relationship management will use the developed techniques to ensure that needs and expectations are met and managed. |
| A service provider may be a consumer in its own right, so it may have relationships with upstream partners and suppliers. Ensuring these relationships are healthy allows the service provider to have confidence in its ability to deliver downstream products and services. |
| The service provider also has to manage non-service-related relationships. Non-service-related relationships that need to be managed include:<br>• *"Government and regulators*<br>• *Society and community*<br>• *Industry and competition* |

## 3: Fostering stakeholder relationships

> - *Shareholders, investors, sponsors*
> - *Media"*
>
> While these groups have different interests to the service group, the relationships still need to be actively managed. Operations will require a level of transparency and good communication is mandatory. Other ITIL practices will be involved in these relationships, specifically portfolio management, business analysis, risk management and strategy management.

> Based on my experience, the most important element of relationship management is remembering that it's a long-term commitment. Just like a personal relationship, we need to dedicate time and effort to stop our professional relationships going stale.
>
> For example, a new supplier relationship might start with monthly service reviews attended by senior people on both sides. Gradually, the senior people start to miss occasional meetings. They send someone more junior, who then becomes their permanent replacement. The junior person starts to skip meetings, and eventually the regular review just drops off the calendar. When something happens and action is required, the lines of communication have been severed.

# 3: Fostering stakeholder relationships

> It can be challenging to balance a busy diary and attending a meeting that doesn't feel essential, but we must commit time to relationships. If meetings aren't the way forward, what other techniques can we use instead? I've seen everything from Kanban boards to newsletters incorporated into a relationship management approach.

## The supplier management practice

The purpose of the supplier management practice is *"to ensure that the organization's suppliers and their performances are managed appropriately to support the seamless provision of quality products and services. This includes creating closer, more collaborative relationships with key suppliers to uncover and realize new value and reduce the risk of failure."*

To be effective, supplier management needs:

- A common approach to sourcing and a sourcing strategy, aligned to the overall organisational strategy;
- Effective supplier relationship management;
- A single point of control over active and planned supplier contracts and services; and
- Policies and guidelines.

Many organisations experience poor supplier performance because their supplier management practice is disconnected. Procurement teams carry out the evaluation and assign contracts, but then management is passed on to another area of the organisation (if it is done at all). Supplier management is essential for organisations in today's environment. Some organisations will outsource supplier management to an external party, although they must retain overall governance.

## 3: Fostering stakeholder relationships

The supplier management practice has close links to other practices, including:

- Relationship management
- Service level management
- Service financial management
- Risk management
- Service configuration management

### Practice success factors

There are three practice success factors for supplier management:

- *"Ensuring that the sourcing strategy and guidelines effectively support the organization's strategy*
- *Ensuring that service relationships with all suppliers and partners are managed effectively and in line with internal and external regulations*
- *Ensuring the effective integration of third-party services into the organization's products and services"*

**Table 21: Support The Organisation's Strategy With The Sourcing Strategy and Guidelines**

| PSF: Support the organisation's strategy with the sourcing strategy and guidelines |
|---|
| Organisations define their sourcing strategy as part of strategy management. This will include the sourcing policy, and principles and criteria for sourcing resources. The sourcing strategy also includes supplier |

## 3: Fostering stakeholder relationships

categorisation, requirements, and rules for supplier management.

The sourcing strategy is supported by guidelines including:

- The management of the service relationship from inception to completion;
- The management of contracts and agreements;
- Supplier performance management and reporting; and
- Integration of third-party services into the organisation's products and services.

To be effective, organisations must be able to:

- Formulate contracts and agreements;
- Evaluate and negotiate contract terms; and
- Review contracts for renewal and/or termination.

Supplier performance must be measured to ensure compliance and value for money.

**Table 22: Effective Service Relationship Management With All Suppliers and Partners**

| PSF: Effective service relationship management with all suppliers and partners |
| --- |
| Different management approaches are required depending on whether a relationship is basic, cooperative or partnership. The more dependent the organisation is on the supplier, the more management effort is required. |

## 3: Fostering stakeholder relationships

> Each organisation will define a set of measures to assess supplier effectiveness, which could include innovation, financial savings, collaboration, conflict handling, and more.

**Table 23: Effective Integration of Third-Party Services**

| PSF: Effective integration of third-party services |
| --- |
| As most organisations now rely to a greater or lesser extent on third-party services, integration becomes a key capability. These areas are critical:<br><br>• Understanding the external service's scope, nature and terms of provision.<br>• Understanding dependencies.<br>• Understanding risks.<br>• Considering dependencies and risks from product inception throughout the whole product lifecycle.<br><br>The supplier management practice will support value streams that include third-party services and components at the operational level. Supplier onboarding and offboarding must follow defined procedures, and dependencies must be mapped and understood. This allows products and service to continue unaffected, even when suppliers are changed or removed. |

# CHAPTER 4: HOW TO SHAPE DEMAND AND DEFINE SERVICE OFFERINGS

This chapter is focused on step 4 of the customer journey: **offer**.

The topics include:

- Methods for designing digital service experiences;
- Approaches for selling and obtaining service offerings;
- How to capture, influence and manage demand and opportunities;
- How to collect, specify and prioritise requirements; and
- How the business analysis practice can be applied to support requirement management and service design.

The offer step allows the service provider and consumer to build on their relationship to shape customer demand and service offerings. This includes qualifying, designing, selling and obtaining products and services based on value-, data- and user-driven design approaches.

Table 24 shows more information on the purpose of shaping demand and service offerings.

## 4: How to shape demand and define service offerings

**Table 24: The Purpose of Shaping Demand and Service Offerings**[31]

| *Offer* | *For the service consumer* | *For the service provider* |
|---|---|---|
| *Facilitate outcome and experience* | *To ensure that the customer articulates the true needs and demands of the service consumer* | *To understand how value is created for and with the service consumer and how the service provider can support this value co-creation* |
| | | *To enable the service provider to balance supply and demand* |
| *Optimize risk and compliance* | *To minimize the risk of buying services and not fulfilling a real need* | *To minimize the risk of promising services they cannot fulfil* |
| | *To reduce the risk that the supplier* | |

---

[31] *ITIL® 4: Drive Stakeholder Value*, table 5.1. Copyright © AXELOS Limited 2020. Used under permission of AXELOS Limited. All rights reserved.

## 4: How to shape demand and define service offerings

|  | misunderstands the consumer's needs | To minimize the risk of unhappy customers |
|---|---|---|
| **Optimize resources and minimize cost** | To ensure money is invested in areas that optimize return of investment | To ensure time and resources are used in the optimum areas |

**Designing digital service experiences**

Digital service design needs to involve customers and users throughout the design and implementation process. Value-driven and data-driven design is an iterative approach based on frequent feedback, learning and building in value co-creation. The service provider and consumer need to engage and communicate all the way through the design process.

This section considers these design-related concepts:

- Lean thinking
- Agile product and service development
- User-centred design
- Service blueprinting
- Designing for onboarding

*Lean thinking*

Lean thinking focuses on the elimination of waste and the voice of the customer as part of process improvement. *"Lean thinking can be described as a process improvement philosophy that prioritizes flow efficiency over resource efficiency. In Lean, flow refers to the manner in which work progresses through a system. A work unit can be defined as*

## 4: How to shape demand and define service offerings

*a piece of work flowing through the value stream."* [If you put a camera on the work unit, a "good flow" means that the work unit moves steadily and predictably, whereas "bad flow" describes a system with a lot of queues with many work items in them, where the work unit will have to stop and wait.]

Lean prioritises the flow of work over focus on individual resources. Key terms include:

- **Flow:** The way work progresses through a system;
- **Work unit:** A piece of work moving through a value stream;
- **Good flow:** Work units move predictably and steadily; and
- **Bad flow:** Workflows do not move predictably and steadily, and queues and bottlenecks occur.

The ITIL 4 guiding principles' focus on value and think and work holistically to support Lean thinking:

**Table 25: The Five Lean Principles**[32]

| | |
|---|---|
| *Identify customer value* | *The first thing is to understand what the customer needs. What creates value for the customer? What is the desired outcome? Why is it needed? When and where* |

---

[32] *ITIL® 4: Drive Stakeholder Value*, table 5.10. Copyright © AXELOS Limited 2020. Used under permission of AXELOS Limited. All rights reserved.

## 4: How to shape demand and define service offerings

|  | is it needed? How much? How frequently? |
|---|---|
| **Map the value stream** | Next is understanding the value stream. From the moment a service provider receives a request from the customer for a new or changed product or service, the required activities need to be designed, built, transitioned, and delivered. The key is to define the work unit (request, product, service) and map how it flows through the value chain. Each flow represents a value stream. |
| **Create flow** | The work unit may be subject to several bottlenecks in the value stream. From the perspective of the work unit, this is waste. The flow is improved by eliminating waste. |
| **Establish pull** | When flow is created, the next step is to optimize the |

## 4: How to shape demand and define service offerings

|  | value stream. This 'pull' principle ensures that work is not pushed downstream. It allows batch size and work in progress to be limited, so that work units are finished in time. |
|---|---|
| **Seek perfection** | This principle reflects continual improvement. |

Why not try applying this to a workflow in your own organisation? For example, the purchase workflow, or onboarding a new customer. Can you identify any opportunities for improvement?

If you can see areas where things can be done better, this is a good test for your overall organisational improvement process. Do you know how to record and act on the improvement opportunity? Does your organisation follow an improvement process?

### *Agile product and service development*

Iterative development relies on feedback to shape the next stage of the project or process. Agile software development

## 4: How to shape demand and define service offerings

is an example of an iterative approach; you can see the Agile manifesto below:

**Table 26: The Agile Manifesto**

| We value... | | |
|---|---|---|
| Individuals and interactions | *Over* | Processes and tools |
| Working product | *Over* | Comprehensive documentation |
| Customer collaboration | *Over* | Contract negotiation |
| Responding to change | *Over* | Following a plan |
| *That is, while there is value in the items on the right, we value the items on the left more.* | | |

### *User-centred design*

User-centred (or centric) design is also an iterative design process, with a primary focus on user experience (UX), rather than focusing on technical or business requirements.

*"UX deals with users interacting with a product or service and the experience they receive from that interaction."*

It is supported by these guiding principles:

- Focus on value.
- Collaborate and promote visibility.

# 4: How to shape demand and define service offerings

- Progress iteratively with feedback.

The steps in the image below are an example of a user-centric design process. They reflect an iterative approach focused on user needs, which would work well with Agile software development.

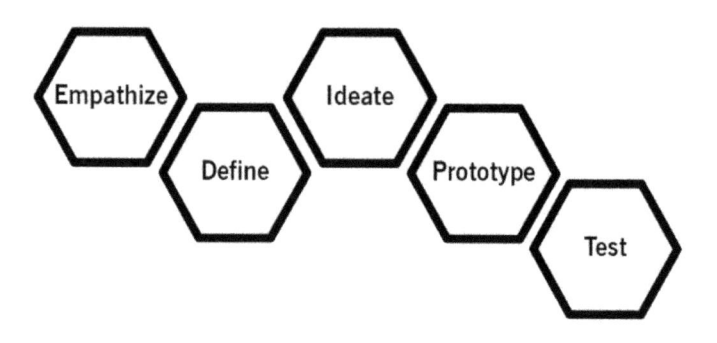

**Figure 16: User-centred design**

## Service blueprinting

A service blueprint is *"a diagram visualizing the service usage, with the aim of optimizing the user experience"*. One service may have multiple blueprints to reflect different scenarios. The key elements of the blueprint are:

- **Line of interaction:** The line of interaction *"pinpoints the direct service interactions between the customer/user and the service provider"*.
- **Line of visibility:** The line of visibility *"separates the service activities that are visible to the customer and users from those that are not visible"*. Every "frontstage" activity appears above this line, while

everything "backstage" (not visible) appears below this line.
- **Line of internal interaction:** The line of internal interaction *"separates the employees in contact from those who do not directly support interactions with customers and users"*.

## Designing for onboarding

User-centred design includes onboarding for each product and service to make sure it happens smoothly. The documented onboarding approach will include:

- Scope
- Actions
- Stakeholders
- Timelines

Key onboarding activities will include:

- Identifying the service provider resources that will interact with the consumer's resources, and vice versa;
- Identifying the need for introducing each pair of resources;
- Exploring opportunities to optimise and automate introductions;
- Creating procedures where manual or human-controlled introduction is required;
- Testing the procedures and updating based on test results; and
- Documenting, and communication to the involved parties.

## 4: How to shape demand and define service offerings

The four dimensions of service management and any external factors need to be considered.

> *"You never get a second chance to make a first impression"* is a common saying. It applies perfectly in the case of onboarding. If a service provider doesn't manage the onboarding process, it will have to work twice as hard to establish a strong relationship with its customer. Equally, the consumer must also work hard during the onboarding process. It needs to provide access to the right people and systems at the right time. If the consumer doesn't fulfil its side of the agreement, it might not get the full value (or return on investment) from its service provider.

### Approaches for selling and obtaining service offerings

Once products and/or services have been designed, they need to be sold (offered) to consumers. The sale may happen before or after the service is built, depending on the type of agreement. Internal and external service providers need to 'sell' services; the activities will vary depending on the type of customer and the nature of the relationship.

Key concepts here are:

- Pricing
- Internal sales

# 4: How to shape demand and define service offerings

- External sales

## *Pricing*

Pricing decides how much the customer will be charged. Viable products and services generate enough income to cover investments and costs, as well as profit if the service provider is a profit-making organisation.

Commercial service providers can price based on the perceived value of a service and the price of other, comparable services. They may also set targets related to profit margin, and the expected lifespan of the product or service.

Pricing options include:

- Cost
- Cost plus
- Market price/going rate
- Fixed price
- Differential charging

You can do more research into the different pricing options if this is relevant for your role.

## *Internal sales*

Internal customers are part of the same organisation as the service provider (for example, an IT department 'selling' to other areas of the business). Internal customers need to be aware of the products and services available to them. Benefits of selling to internal customers include:

- Better use of existing services;
- Better management of service demand;

## 4: How to shape demand and define service offerings

- Better communication with customers and users; and
- Better access to feedback about products and services.

The service catalogue is an important tool for internal sales, helping ensure customers understand what is available to them and how to request access.

These ITIL practices provide more information on internal sales:

- Relationship management
- Service catalogue management
- Service desk
- Service level management
- Service request management

### External sales

External selling uses traditional techniques that you will be familiar with, like advertising and sales campaigns. The sales process will depend on factors including:

- Any regulation or legislation that is applicable, for example in the public sector;
- Whether consumers purchase directly, or via a procurement function; and
- The type of process that must be followed, for example tendering processes, proof of concept, etc.

Value co-creation and a successful sales process rely on good communication, trust and fairness on both sides. The service provider shouldn't unnecessarily inflate the price, and the service consumer shouldn't try to achieve a price reduction that will make the service non-viable for the provider. The

# 4: How to shape demand and define service offerings

service provider should listen to its consumer, and the consumer should present requirements, rather than assume it knows the exact solution it needs.

## Managing demand and opportunities

Services cannot be 'stored' for later use like goods can. Demand and capacity are connected, and spikes in demand can cause performance degradation and service interruption. Service providers need to be able to adjust capacity and influence demand, by understanding their customer groups and segments and by creating scalable products and services.

Key concepts here include how to:

- Understand patterns of business activity;
- Optimise capacity;
- Shape or smooth demand;
- Build the customer business case; and
- Build the service provider business case.

### *Patterns of business activity*

A pattern of business activity (PBA) is *"a workload profile of one or more business activities. PBAs are used to help the service provider understand and support different levels of service consumer activity."*

Service providers should analyse patterns of business activity.

## 4: How to shape demand and define service offerings

> What patterns of business activity are Banksbest likely to see? Think about the Bizbank service. For example, perhaps Banksbest will see an increase in demand for custom reports at financial year end. Can you think of any other daily, weekly, monthly or annual patterns it should expect?

### Optimising capacity

Figure 17[33] shows the relationship between demand, capacity and supply.

---

[33] *ITIL® 4: Drive Stakeholder Value*, figure 5.1. Copyright © AXELOS Limited 2020. Used under permission of AXELOS Limited. All rights reserved.

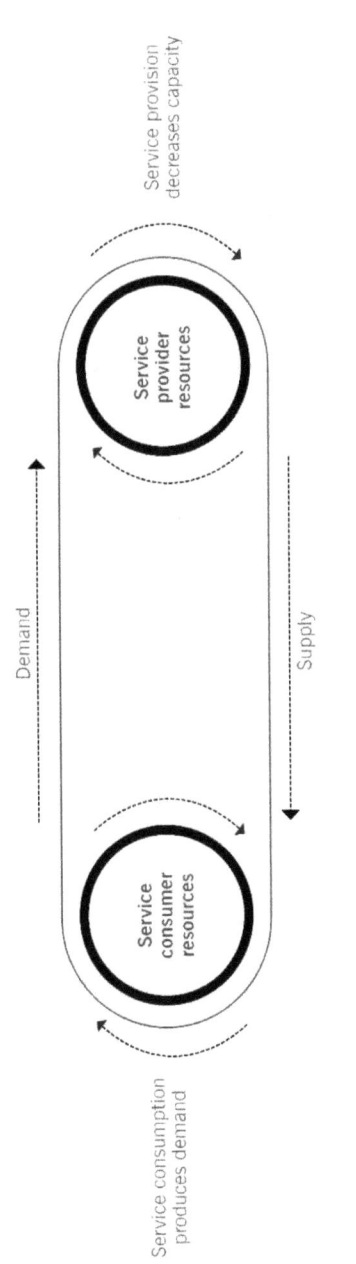

## 4: How to shape demand and define service offerings

**Figure 17: Relationship between demand, capacity, and supply**

## 4: How to shape demand and define service offerings

Both capacity and demand need to be managed.

- Demand management focuses on understanding user profiles and/or personas and influencing their behaviour.
- Capacity and performance management focuses on providing the right level of capacity to respond to changing demand. This can include increasing capacity during peak times, reducing capacity when workload reduces, moving jobs during peak hours and introducing freeze periods when changes are not allowed.

Demand can be fixed or variable.

The capacity and performance management practice has three perspectives:

- **Business capacity management:** plans for capacity triggered by the customer.
- **Product and service capacity management:** manages end-to-end product or service capacity.
- **Component capacity management:** monitors and tunes product and service components that can affect the overall product or service.

The four dimensions of service management can also be used as a lens to view capacity management.

Digital services allow some activities and capacity to be transferred to the consumer, for example self-check-in for flights and hotels.

### Shaping and smoothing demand

Service providers need to be careful when manipulating pricing to change consumer behaviour. They should ask:

# 4: How to shape demand and define service offerings

- Are the behaviour changes optimising value for both parties?
- Do the mechanisms support optimal resource usage?
- Are there incentives in place for both parties?

Consumers do not like to feel they are being taken advantage of by unfair price changes.

The data from capacity and performance management and demand management activities can identify improvement opportunities for products and services, for example:

- Service usage analysis;
- Incident and problem analysis;
- Analysis of service request patterns;
- Usage of knowledge articles;
- User feedback;
- Increased or decreased service demand; and
- Market changes, new technologies.

---

Effective demand and capacity management relies on information from the entire organisation, and is supported by good communication between teams.

In the UK, an online gambling portal experienced the negative consequences of poor demand management. Within the organisation, the marketing team built a campaign to encourage new sign-ups with an offer to

# 4: How to shape demand and define service offerings

> match people's first bet amount. The offer was very popular, but unfortunately no one had told the IT department about what was planned. The spike in traffic led to slow and patchy performance on the website, creating a poor onboarding experience.
>
> You may have similar stories from your own experience.

## Building the customer business case

A business case is *"a justification for the expenditure of organizational resources, providing information about costs, benefits, options, risks and issues"*.

The business case should provide financial analysis to support any change.

The customer will need to create a business case to address demand through new or changed services. The following tables provide more information about the business case and typical areas of conflict and uncertainty.

**Table 27: Examples of Typical Areas of Conflict and Uncertainty**[34]

| Areas for investigation | Typical examples of conflicting areas within an organization |
|---|---|
| Value<br>Understanding real needs | Who are the key stakeholders, and how are their needs prioritized? |

---

[34] *ITIL® 4: Drive Stakeholder Value*, table 5.4. Copyright © AXELOS Limited 2020. Used under permission of AXELOS Limited. All rights reserved.

## 4: How to shape demand and define service offerings

|  |  | The users of the service may have different needs and priorities from the customer/sponsor (see Table 5.5). Other stakeholder groups may also have conflicting needs. |
|---|---|---|
| Outcome | **Understanding benefits** | It may be tempting to focus solely on short-term benefits at the expense of longer-term benefits. On the other hand, long-term benefits are typically subject to more uncertainty and risk. |
| Cost | **Understanding capital and operating expenses** | What kind of investment do we need for this product or service? What is the implementation cost? What is the maintenance and support cost? What is the cost of usage? How much training is needed? What kind of organizational change is needed? |
| Risk | **Understanding uncertainty and impact** | It is difficult to know in advance whether a service provider is willing and able to fulfil the needs of the service consumer. It is important to establish a good relationship from the start, not only with the sales people, but also with the people who will be key resources for service provision. It is good to include incentives for relationship building and a win-win culture in agreements and contracts. |

# 4: How to shape demand and define service offerings

**Table 28: Conflicting Customer and User Priorities and Needs[35]**

| Customers | Users | Conflict | To consider |
|---|---|---|---|
| **Cost** <br><br> Is it cost-effective? Does it compare with similar services from other providers? Can anything be cut to make it cheaper? | **Performance** <br><br> How fast is it? How quick is response time? Will it be there when I need it? How convenient is it to use? What emotions does it trigger? | The better the performance, the more expensive the service. | A decision to go with a cheaper service should be balanced with the costs of: <br><br> • worse performance <br> • negative user experience. |
| **Profitability/ value** <br><br> Will this service provide a return on investment? Will it help us to meet | **Ease of use** <br><br> How intuitive is the user interface? How many screens do I have to go through to complete a transaction? | Ease of use may require additional investments. | Ease of use will increase profitability over time. It will enable users to meet organizational goals and minimize the need for |

---

[35] *ITIL® 4: Drive Stakeholder Value*, table 5.5. Copyright © AXELOS Limited 2020. Used under permission of AXELOS Limited. All rights reserved.

## 4: How to shape demand and define service offerings

| our business objectives? | Will it make my job easier? |  | training and support. |
|---|---|---|---|
| **Service impact** <br><br> What will this service actually achieve? Will it increase productivity? Will it enable the improvement of services? <br><br> Where will the organization be in the future? | **Quality** <br><br> How does this service actually work? Will it do everything it needs [to] do? Will training be available? Will it solve problems? | Customers are not as concerned about service quality as long as it does the job at a reasonable price. | If it is difficult for the user to achieve high quality, there will be negative impacts for the business: <br><br> • worse performance <br> • more errors made by users <br> • errors and corrections. |
| **Innovation** <br><br> Will this service enable opportunity identification and help to grow the business? Will it open new markets? | **Consistency** <br><br> Will the service be available to use for the duration of employment? | Customers may have strategic concerns that are of little interest to users. | With the help of IT services, many routine tasks can be automated, enabling staff to focus more on innovation. |

# 4: How to shape demand and define service offerings

| Will it enable delivery expansion? | | | |
|---|---|---|---|

## *Building the service provider business case*

The service provider also needs a profitable and viable business case for it to continue operating in the future. The service provider needs to consider the customer's business case (if available) as it builds its own business case. The service provider must understand the cost of providing a service so there are no surprises in the future.

The ITIL practices that can provide input to the service provider business case include:

- Availability management
- Capacity and performance management
- Information security management
- Portfolio management
- Relationship management
- Service continuity management
- Service financial management

## Managing requirements

The customer and the service provider need to work together in an open and transparent way to define requirements (part of the 'band of visibility'). Requirements can evolve during the development process, and many organisations use business analysts to help them elicit and analyse requirements. The techniques in this lesson are used by business analysts as part of the business analysis practice.

# 4: How to shape demand and define service offerings

Business analysis is *"the practice of analysing a business or some element of a business, defining its needs and recommending solutions to address these needs and/or solve a business problem, and create value for stakeholders. Business analysis enables an organization to communicate its needs in a meaningful way, express the rationale for change, and design and describe solutions that enable value creation in alignment with the organization's objectives."*

Key topics here include:

- Understanding roles and responsibilities;
- Managing requirements;
- Separating the problem from the solution;
- Using a minimum viable product;
- User stories and mapping;
- MoSCoW; and
- Weighting.

## *Understanding roles and responsibilities*

Figure 18 shows the roles involved in transforming needs into requirements.

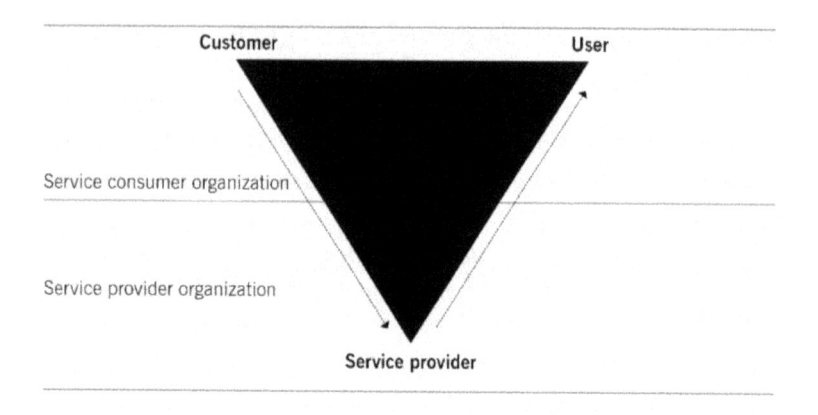

## 4: How to shape demand and define service offerings

**Figure 18: The service delivery triangle: the roles involved in transforming needs into requirements**[36]

Understanding roles and responsibilities supports effective requirements management. It is important to identify the right contributors, and capture, articulate and represent user needs and expectations. In larger organisations, customers and users may be different groups. Requirements need to be negotiated and agreed between the service provider and the customer, and expectations need to be managed.

Table 29 shows more information about service consumer roles and requirements specification.

---

[36] *ITIL® 4: Drive Stakeholder Value*, figure 5.2. Copyright © AXELOS Limited 2020. Used under permission of AXELOS Limited. All rights reserved.

## 4: How to shape demand and define service offerings

**Table 29: Examples of Service Consumer Roles and Requirement Specification Scenarios[37]**

| Scenario | Involved roles |
|---|---|
| A customer orders a pre-defined standard service/product from a service provider, such as a laptop, smartphone, or app. | The customer selects the standard service from a service provider based on a requirement specification. Representative users are consulted as part of the requirement specification. Based on their individual requirements, the users then choose between pre-defined alternatives. |
| A customer obtains an off-the-shelf service from a provider to be configured, implemented, and managed internally in the service consumer organization. | The customer conducts a proper evaluation upfront, to ensure a service that fits the needs of the service consumer. The customer evaluates whether it is fit for purpose and use. Even though it is an off-the-shelf service, there may still be many configuration options. Representative users of the service are therefore involved in the requirement |

---

[37] *ITIL® 4: Drive Stakeholder Value*, table 5.6. Copyright © AXELOS Limited 2020. Used under permission of AXELOS Limited. All rights reserved.

## 4: How to shape demand and define service offerings

|  | specification and implementation. |
|---|---|
|  | Other stakeholders, such as an internal IT department, contribute with non-functional requirements for the architectural fit and integration with existing infrastructure. |
| *A service provider develops a new and innovative service for or on behalf of a customer.* | *To successfully develop a complex new service, an Agile approach to requirements specification is considered in order to:*<br><br>• *iteratively break down complexity*<br>• *build in technical requirements, such as security, from the start*<br>• *involve the customer and ensure frequent feedback loops.*<br><br>*This approach requires active customer participation throughout product development. For success, it is important that the customer (for example, a product owner) has the authority to make decisions on behalf of the service* |

## 4: How to shape demand and define service offerings

|  | consumer on requirements and prioritization. Users may be consulted or even involved in kick-offs, demos, etc. |
|---|---|
| *A service provider designs a new commodity service for the mass market.* | *Requirements are owned and managed by the service provider, who may or may not involve the service consumers in the transformation of needs into requirements.* |

### Managing requirements

Requirements must be specified, managed and tracked. The requirement owner role will:

- Identify stakeholder groups and representatives;
- Help representatives to articulate requirements on behalf of their stakeholder groups;
- Collect, document, manage, track and communicate requirements;
- Ensure requirements are interpreted and understood correctly; and
- Validate products and services against requirements.

Requirements will evolve and change throughout the product or service design process. Requirements need to adapt and must be testable to ensure they are aligned with customer needs.

## 4: How to shape demand and define service offerings

**Utility** (fit for purpose) requirements cover data, information and functionality. **Warranty** (fit for use) requirements cover:

- *"Usability*
- *Availability and reliability*
- *Capacity and performance*
- *Information security*
- *Compliance*
- *Continuity*
- *Maintainability*
- *Operability*
- *Measurability and reportability*
- *Scalability"*

> Using the case study, create a list of requirements for the biometrics element that is planned for the My Way service.
>
> What utility requirements could there be? And what warranty requirements?

### *Separating the problem from the solution*

Customers sometimes specify a solution, rather than a problem. They might say, for example, "I saw this amazing product at a tradeshow, and it will solve all our issues!"

## 4: How to shape demand and define service offerings

Service providers need requirements that separate the problem from the solution to be sure the customer gets what they need, not what they think they want. This is a delicate process and it takes time to elicit the full requirements.

> One of the challenges I've faced with requirements gathering is the tendency for the list of requirements to get out of control. Faced with seemingly limitless possibilities, users let their imagination roam and can really surprise you!
>
> This isn't a bad thing, but it can make expectation setting more difficult. This is why it's good to focus on outcomes before getting too far into the detail of requirements. Once both parties have a very clear understanding of what exactly the product or service needs to do, it is much easier to link requirements to outcomes and see which have a higher priority or broader applicability.

### *Minimum viable product*

A minimum viable product (MVP) is *"a product with just enough features to satisfy early customers and to provide feedback for future product development"*.

The concept of an MVP is widely used in Agile development, with each set of feedback being used to adjust requirements and support the next iteration.

## 4: How to shape demand and define service offerings

### User stories and story mapping

A user story is *"a way of representing areas of functionality required by the stakeholders in a way that generates discussion and understanding among team members, helping them to work together to turn requirements into working products and services. User stories are used to describe fragments of a product or service."*

User stories should be specific and simple. An epic describes the bigger picture for a product or service; this can then be broken down into user stories and mapped. Figure 19 shows an example of story mapping.

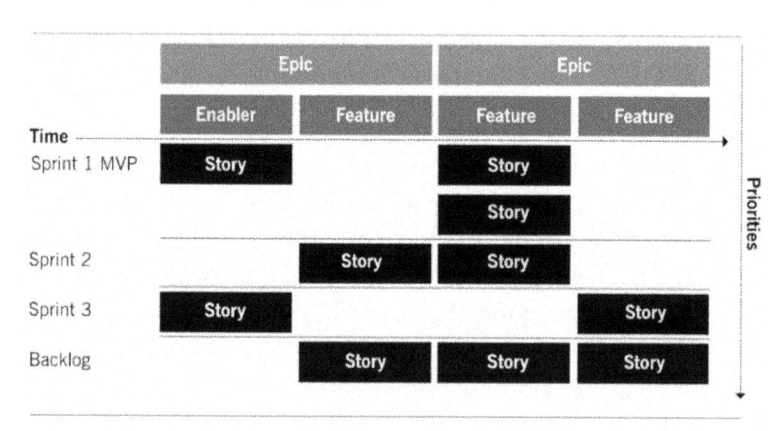

**Figure 19: An example of story mapping**[38]

Table 30 contains more details about story mapping.

---

[38] *ITIL® 4: Drive Stakeholder Value*, figure 5.3. Copyright © AXELOS Limited 2020. Used under permission of AXELOS Limited. All rights reserved.

## 4: How to shape demand and define service offerings

**Table 30: Using Epics, Features, Enablers, and Stories To Articulate Requirements**[39]

| Type | Description | Example |
|---|---|---|
| *Epics* | *An epic is an initiative delivering new products, services, or customer journeys to customers.* <br><br> *The epic is the large story or a user story, which is too big to cover in one sprint.* <br><br> *Epics are comprised of large collections of features.* | *The entire user experience from hiring a car to delivering it.* |
| *Features /enablers* | *A feature is a collection of related user stories that represent a whole area of* | *A busy manager can pick up the car at the airport to reach a meeting.* |

---

[39] *ITIL® 4: Drive Stakeholder Value*, table 5.9. Copyright © AXELOS Limited 2020. Used under permission of AXELOS Limited. All rights reserved.

## 4: How to shape demand and define service offerings

|  | | |
|---|---|---|
|  | *functionality or a capability that a product or service owner is interested in.* <br><br> *A feature is realized by some number of user stories.* <br><br> *An enabler is a technical prerequisite for a feature that supports exploration, architecture, infrastructure, or compliance.* | |
| **User stories/enabler stories** | *A piece of functionality described in a way that could be developed in a single sprint.* <br><br> *As a <user> I want <requirement> so that <benefit>.* | *A busy manager can order fast-track pickup at the airport to reduce stress.* <br><br> *A busy manager can leave the airport without paying a parking fee to reduce waiting time.* |

# 4: How to shape demand and define service offerings

The common user story format is:

**As role, I want feature/what, so that why.**

Use the INVEST acronym to support your user stories. They should be independent, negotiable, valuable, estimable, small, testable.

## *MoSCoW*

The MoSCoW method is used as a prioritisation technique for requirements management. Stakeholders can agree on priorities and highlight anything that won't be delivered. This helps to identify and reduce requirements that are adding costs, but not adding value.

MoSCoW stands for:

- **Must** – mandatory requirements.
- **Should** – requirements to be included if possible.
- **Could** – requirements that could be included if they don't affect 'should' or 'must' requirements.
- **Won't** – requirements that won't be included at this time.

## *Weighting*

If a product or service has many requirements with the same MoSCoW rating, more granular prioritisation is needed. There are many different approaches, one of which is weighted shortest job first (WSJF). The weight of a job is divided by the duration or size. Cost of delay is a recommended measure to use for digital products and services. Figure 20 shows how the cost of delay is scored and then prioritised according to CD3: cost of delay divided by duration.

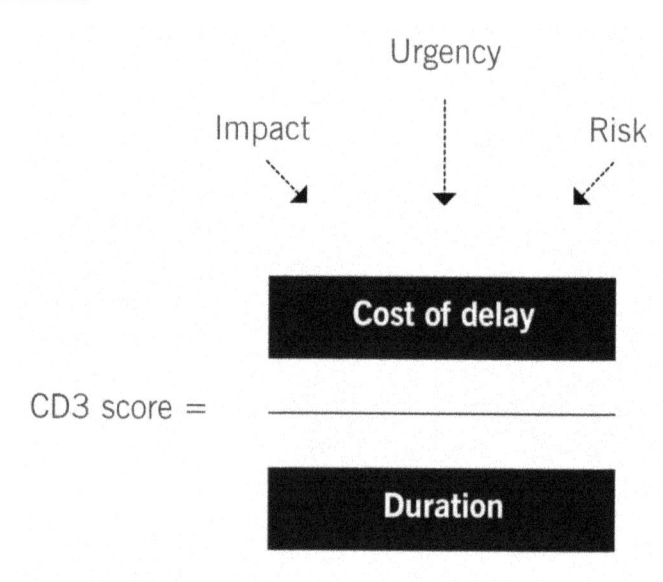

**Figure 20: Cost of delay divided by duration adapted to service management terms**[40]

## The business analysis practice

The purpose of the business analysis practice is to *"analyze a part or the entirety of a business, define its needs, and recommend solutions to address these needs and/or solve a business problem. The solutions must facilitate value creation for the stakeholders. Business analysis enables an organization to communicate its needs in a meaningful way and express the rationale for change. This practice enables*

---

[40] *ITIL® 4: Drive Stakeholder Value*, figure 5.4. Copyright © AXELOS Limited 2020. Used under permission of AXELOS Limited. All rights reserved.

## 4: How to shape demand and define service offerings

an organization to design and describe solutions that enable value relation, in alignment with the organization's objectives."

The practice enables meaningful communication, the ability to express the reason for change, and the design of solutions for value creation. The needs of both the customer and the organisation are identified and addressed so an appropriate solution is deployed. Business analysis also ensures that the solutions are cost-effective.

As organisations move to a more digital orientation, Agile practices are becoming more embedded in business operations. Digital organisations need a stronger tie to the strategic initiatives, customer and user experience, exploitation of technology, business process re-evaluation, and an acceptance of digital business architecture. Working in an Agile manner, small, specialised work groups are now using the business analyst as a product or service owner. As digital solutions are more closely linked to the business value stream, business analysis moves from being an intermediary to an *"integrated business practice"*.

### Practice success factors

Two practice success factors (PSFs) have been defined for the business analysis practice:

*"Establishing and continually improving an organization-wide approach to business analysis to ensure that it is conducted in a consistent and effective manner.*

*Ensuring that current and future needs of the organization and its customers are understood, analyzed, and supported with timely, efficient, and effective solution proposals."*

## 4: How to shape demand and define service offerings

**Table 31: PSF: Establish and Continually Improve An Organisation-wide Approach To Business Analysis**

| PSF: Establish and continually improve an organisation-wide approach to business analysis |
|---|
| Consistency is vital within a business analysis practice, but consistency doesn't mean every task needs to be performed in the same manner. The context of the task will dictate the model that is required. For example, consider the difference between an Agile environment and a traditional waterfall approach. |
| Business analysis is a "thoughtful" practice – tasks include the objective analysis of information for wise business investments. Skills include data modelling, and analysing organisational structure, processes, scope and decision making. |

**Table 32: PSF: Ensure The Current and Future Needs of The Organisation and Its Customers Are Understood and Supported**

| PSF: Ensure the current and future needs of the organisation and its customers are understood and supported |
|---|
| Business analysis translates ideas into solutions. Not only do ideas need to be communicated clearly but the recipient must also have the steps necessary to deploy the idea. Ideas are communicated with two intents:<br>• Customers needing a solution to fulfil a need, typically via business case. |

*4: How to shape demand and define service offerings*

- Service provider's teams that design, develop and deliver the solution, based on documented requirements, recommendations and priorities.

The skills needed for good business analysis include emotional intelligence and service empathy.

# CHAPTER 5: HOW TO ALIGN EXPECTATIONS AND AGREE SERVICE DETAILS

This chapter is focused on step 4 of the customer journey: **agree**.

Key topics include:

- How to plan for value co-creation;
- How to negotiate and agree service utility, warranty and experience; and
- How the service level management practice contributes to service expectation management.

The agree step aligns expectations and ensures a shared view of the service scope and quality between provider and consumer. Agree may include contractual agreement with involvement from stakeholders including legal and procurement teams. Agreed targets will be reviewed over time as the service evolves and customer needs change.

Table 33 shows more information on the purpose of aligning expectations and agreeing services.

## 5: How to align expectations and agree service details

**Table 33: The Purpose of Aligning Expectations and Agreeing Services**[41]

| Agree | *For the service consumer* | *For the service provider* |
|---|---|---|
| Facilitate outcome and experience | *To ensure that services provided meet customers' and users' requirements and expectations*<br><br>*To increase potential value from services and service relationship*<br><br>*To ensure a shared understanding of service quality among all stakeholders*<br><br>*To ensure a shared understanding of responsibilities of the stakeholders* | *To ensure a shared understanding of service quality among all involved stakeholders*<br><br>*To ensure a shared understanding of responsibilities of the stakeholders*<br><br>*To ensure realistic expectations from services and service relationship*<br><br>*To increase potential value from service delivery and service relationship* |

---

[41] *ITIL® 4: Drive Stakeholder Value*, table 6.1. Copyright © AXELOS Limited 2020. Used under permission of AXELOS Limited. All rights reserved.

## 5: How to align expectations and agree service details

| | | |
|---|---|---|
| Optimize risk and compliance | To ensure sufficient control of service quality and transparency of services' status<br><br>To counteract misunderstandings and misalignments between the parties involved<br><br>To reduce the risk of non-compliance<br><br>To ensure a shared understanding of service-related risks<br><br>To arrange compensating controls for risks that cannot be shared or transferred through agreements | To counteract misunderstandings and misalignments between the parties involved<br><br>To reduce the risk of non-compliance<br><br>To ensure a shared understanding of service-related risks<br><br>To ensure a shared understanding of service price and associated payments, and reduce risks of payment disputes or delays |
| Optimize resources and minimize cost | To ensure a shared understanding of service consumption costs and associated payments<br><br>To optimize service consumption costs | To ensure a shared understanding of service provision costs<br><br>To optimize service provision costs |

## 5: How to align expectations and agree service details

|  | To optimize cost of negotiation and agreement and overall resource utilization | To ensure a shared understanding of service price and associated payments |
|  |  | To optimize cost of negotiation and agreement and overall resource utilization |

**Value co-creation, negotiations and agreement**

The service provider and consumer need a shared understanding of how value will be co-created, tracked, assessed and evaluated. This agreement will then define service measures and reports.

Key topics for this section include:

- Types of service value drivers;
- Service interaction method;
- Inherent and assigned characteristics of services;
- Converting service consumer needs into an agreement; and
- Negotiating and agreeing utility, warranty and experience.

## 5: How to align expectations and agree service details

Many of the service provider relationships I've entered into through my own businesses start with a conversation with a salesperson or an account manager. At the end of the conversation, we both feel like we've got a good understanding of what's needed, and if we agree to proceed, the next step is often a hugely complicated contract covering every eventuality. Once a service starts, it often becomes apparent that some details have been misunderstood and ongoing changes are needed.

One technique I recommend is working together on a 'key facts' document to supplement the contract. This is a less comprehensive summary of the main points and can help to bridge the gap between conversation and contract. We've even had a key facts version of our online terms and conditions drawn up to help people who don't have the time (or desire) to read our full T&Cs. Of course, it's important to get these checked over by your legal representative.

### *Types of service value drivers*

In the ITIL 4 service value system, service consumer objectives are achieved, which fulfil service consumer purposes. Service performance enables service consumer performance, through the utility and warranty of the product or service.

## 5: How to align expectations and agree service details

Service offerings usually have three types of service performance drivers:

- Goods transferred from provider to consumer.
- The service consumer accesses the service provider's resources.
- Service actions are performed by the service provider and/or service users.

Technology-based services usually include access to a service provider's resources and may include service actions. Resources are easy to identify, measure and agree. Service actions can be more challenging to define and measure.

Table 34 shows examples of service value drivers.

**Table 34: Examples of Value Drivers For Different Types of Service Offerings**[42]

| Service example | Transfer of goods | Access to resources | Service actions |
|---|---|---|---|
| Corporate accounting | N/A | Employees in the financial department gain access to: the accounting application with agreed functionality; | User action: any transaction or enquiry in the accounting system through the application |

---

[42] *ITIL® 4: Drive Stakeholder Value*, table 6.2. Copyright © AXELOS Limited 2020. Used under permission of AXELOS Limited. All rights reserved.

## 5: How to align expectations and agree service details

| Service example | Transfer of goods | Access to resources | Service actions |
|---|---|---|---|
| | | the financial and other data of agreed quality; and the service desk and other support interfaces | Service provider action: regularly update consolidated data from different business units<br><br>Joint action: registration of user-reported incidents by service desk agents |
| Broadband internet service for an individual consumer | A wi-fi router and user manual are sold to the user with the ownership rights | Access to local and wide area networks at agreed speeds is provided to all users authorized by the customer<br><br>Access to the user interface for payments, reporting, | User actions: check account status; change the subscription; administer user accounts<br><br>Service provider action: send an invoice to the customer<br><br>Joint action: change the address of the service |

## 5: How to align expectations and agree service details

| Service example | Transfer of goods | Access to resources | Service actions |
|---|---|---|---|
|  |  | and management of the service is provided to the customer | provision when the customer moves to a new place |
| Card payment processing for a small coffee shop | A card reader device is transferred to the customer with the ownership rights | Access to the payment processing service, integrated with the customer's cash register and bank account<br><br>Access to a mobile app for receiving and managing payments<br><br>Access to a support hotline | User actions: receive a card or device payment; cancel a payment; reset the device; pair with a smartphone<br><br>Service provider action: inform the customer about the app updates and other important events<br><br>Joint action: replace a faulty card reader device |

## 5: How to align expectations and agree service details

| Service example | Transfer of goods | Access to resources | Service actions |
|---|---|---|---|
| Infrastructure platform service for product development teams provided by an internal IT infrastructure team | N/A | Access to platform as a service | User actions: install and update applications; configure resources and install, commission, start, stop, and decommission platform components through a standardized interface<br><br>Service provider actions: monitor and report service levels; patch components; invoice the customer<br><br>Joint actions: perform major updates to the platform; solve shared problems |

# 5: How to align expectations and agree service details

## Service interaction method

The service interaction method is a way of describing and evaluating the service outcome, based on service interactions performed by the users and service provider during service consumption. The method includes:

- Identifying service interactions, including service provider, consumer and joint actions;
- Matching service interactions with the service catalogue;
- Agreeing on a service interaction performance target; and
- Agreeing metrics and measures for the services.

Service interactions can be identified by mapping service provider and consumer value streams. If there are no current value stream maps, data can be drawn from other organisational documents and standards. Service interaction identification and agreement will include stakeholders such as:

- Service and/or product owners
- Customer(s)
- Architects
- Business analysts
- Service catalogue manager

## Service characteristics

What does quality look like? Organisations need to define service quality and associated service levels to measure quality.

## 5: How to align expectations and agree service details

Service quality is *"the totality of a service's characteristics that are relevant to its ability to satisfy stated and implied needs"*. A service level is *"one or more metrics that define expected or achieved service quality"*.

Services can be defined using inherent (resource based) and assigned (service/service offering based) characteristics. The service provider decides which characteristics to include in service quality specifications, and which are associated with service delivery.

Inherent characteristics could include:

- *"Functionality and performance*
- *Architecture*
- *Interfaces and compatibility*
- *Costs"*

Assigned characteristics could include:

- *"Price*
- *Risks and compliance*
- *Monitoring*
- *Reporting*
- *Flexibility"*
- Etc.

### From needs to agreement

Defined service consumer needs form the basis of the consumer/provider agreement. Service quality needs to be negotiated, and the negotiations will be affected by factors including:

- Whether the relationship is internal or external;

## 5: How to align expectations and agree service details

- The size of the organisations involved, and level of formality associated;
- If the services are basic or strategic; and
- The level of service customisation that is possible.

Figure 21 shows how the negotiation will narrow down the scope of the service quality characteristics, focusing on what is important and can be measured.

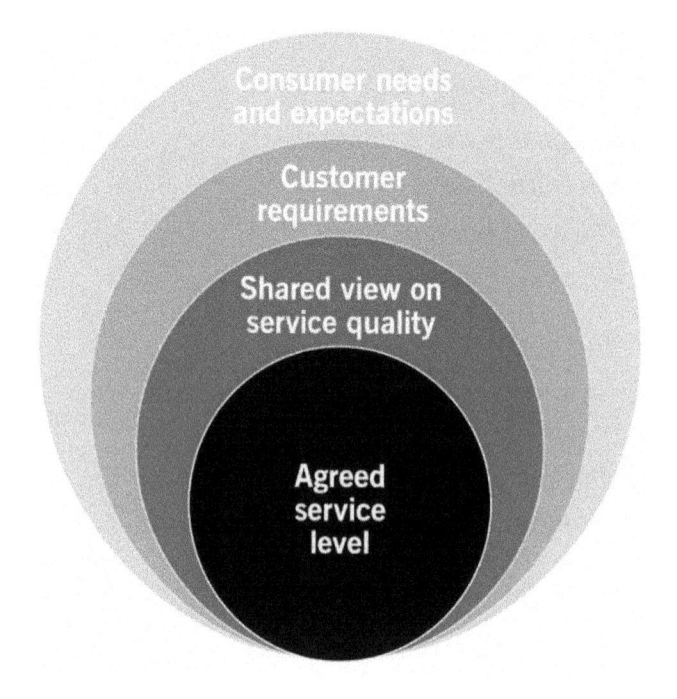

**Figure 21: Limitation of agreements: from the service consumer needs to agreement**[43]

---

[43] *ITIL® 4: Drive Stakeholder Value*, figure 6.1. Copyright © AXELOS Limited 2020. Used under permission of AXELOS Limited. All rights reserved.

# 5: How to align expectations and agree service details

It's much better to have a concise, precise set of targets that can be measured and reported on. Having a huge range of measures makes it challenging to see what really matters. The customer will express their needs and expectations, which can then be distilled into requirements, working together with the service provider. The service provider's input is then included to create a shared view of what 'service quality' looks like. This includes the customer requirements and what the service provider is confident it can deliver and measure.

The targets that form this shared view of service quality then form the basis of the agreed service level. This will be measured and is likely to change and evolve over time as the customer requirements and the service provider's capabilities change and evolve.

---

At Banksbest, part of Doug Range's role is to train the customer service centre staff. What targets would you expect a customer service centre to use to measure quality? Think about both qualitative and quantitative measures, and how you would collect the data.

---

**Negotiating and agreeing utility, warranty and experience**

A service level agreement (SLA) is a *"documented agreement between a service provider and a customer that*

## 5: How to align expectations and agree service details

*identifies both the services required and the expected level of service"*.

A simple SLA includes these three areas:

- **Service** – description and scope.
- **Level** – including metrics and targets for each characteristic.
- **Agreement** – terms and conditions for service provision and consumption.

SLAs may be very simple or, sometimes, very complex; they should be reviewed regularly to ensure they remain fit for purpose. SLAs usually include agreed targets for utility and warranty.

Utility is the functionality the product or service offers – whether it is 'fit for purpose'. Utility is often described in a binary way – it works, or it doesn't work. Warranty is the assurance a product or service will meet agreed requirements – whether it is 'fit for use'. Warranty is not described in a binary way, for example performance may be 'slow' or 'degraded' as well as available or unavailable.

Service providers need to negotiate and agree targets for utility, warranty and experience with their consumers. Effective SLAs should be holistic, yet written in a simple (and often, non-technical) manner to ensure that they are clearly understood by both service provider and customer. For example, an SLA that contains an uptime goal can be meaningless to a customer who doesn't understand how to interpret this statistic or how it's calculated. All of this is focused on delivering value co-creation and fulfilling customer needs.

## 5: How to align expectations and agree service details

Many organisations are now trying to agree and measure targets associated with user experience (UX). UX is *"the sum of functional and emotional interactions with a service and service provider as perceived by a user"*.

For digital services, user experience metrics could include:

- User errors
- Unfinished service interactions
- Cancellations at the end of a trial period
- Etc.

**The service level management practice**

The service level management practice creates and manages a shared view of quality services between the service provider and consumer. The practice purpose is:

*"to set clear business-based targets for service levels, and to ensure that delivery of services is properly assessed, monitored, and managed against these targets."*

The shared view is documented (normally in a service level agreement) and the focus is on service quality and value. Service agreements are in place throughout the entire service relationship, and may need to be updated as the relationship progresses and requirements evolve.

*Practice success factors*

There are four practice success factors (PSFs) for service level management. The PSFs are:

- *"Establishing a shared view of target service levels with customers*

## 5: How to align expectations and agree service details

- *Overseeing how the organization meets the defined service levels through the collection, analysis, storage, and reporting of the relevant metrics for the identified services*
- *Performing service reviews to ensure that the current set of services continues to meet the needs of the organization and its customers*
- *Capturing and reporting on improvement opportunities, including performance against defined service levels and stakeholder satisfaction."*

**Table 35: PSF: Establishing a Shared View of Target Service Levels With Customers**

| PSF: Establishing a shared view of target service levels with customers |
|---|
| Customer interactions will differ depending on the service relationship model – consider, for example, the difference between a tailored/customised relationship and an 'out of the box' relationship. The 'out of the box' customer will need to accept the available services (or have minimal negotiation) while a tailored service offers great flexibility. |
| In a **tailored** service, there is great flexibility in defining the service level targets. However, these targets still need agreement before the service is delivered and consumed. To establish a tailored service, customer needs and expectations form the basis of the discussions about service quality. It is important to ensure that both the customer, including users and sponsors, and service provider, represented by service delivery teams, service |

## 5: How to align expectations and agree service details

provision sponsors, service architects, service designers, business analysist, and service development teams, can agree to the service specifications. As these discussions progress, the scope of service quality is refined and narrowed until it represents a service level that can be delivered at the necessary levels of assurance and liability.

In **'out of the box'** services, service levels are typically predefined. These definitions come from analysing the market to create a generic profile need for that specific service. There might be a tiered set of service delivery options (gold, silver, bronze) for those who wish to use (and pay for) additional functionality.

Regardless of the type of relationship, all agreed service levels should have a clear method for measurement and reporting. If possible, define the metrics early and ensure that measurement and reporting tools are integrated into the service. Metrics that measure overall service quality include functionality, availability, performance, timeliness, user support, accuracy and UX measures.

What happens when the agreed service level quality differs from the expected quality levels? This is where good relationship management skills are needed. The ITIL guiding principles can also help develop a mutually shared view of service quality.

## 5: How to align expectations and agree service details

**Table 36: PSF: Overseeing How the Organisation Meets Service Levels**

| PSF: Overseeing how the organisation meets service levels |
| --- |
| Once the service level targets are established, services are being delivered and consumed. The service provider should control the quality of the service keeping in mind these three views:<br><br>• Achieved service level – compared to what was agreed.<br>• User satisfaction – such as feedback from the service desk, surveys, etc.<br>• Customer satisfaction – such as feedback from reviews, surveys, social media comments, etc.<br><br>The service provider will collect, store, analyse and report on this data to relevant stakeholders for both the provider and consumer. The service level management practice does **not** usually design or execute data collection. Other practices, specifically service design, monitoring and event management, and measuring and reporting, will perform this work. The service level management practice will make sense of the data and then communicate and review it with stakeholders. |

## 5: How to align expectations and agree service details

**Table 37: PSF: Performing Service Reviews**

| PSF: Performing service reviews |
|---|
| The purpose of a service review is to share the achieved service quality and value enabled by the service. As a result, service improvements may be initiated. Service reviews can be one of two types: event based or interval based.<br><br>An event-based review is triggered by events (for example, major incidents, a request for a significant change to a service, a change in business need, etc.). An interval-based review is scheduled at regular and agreed periods. The interval between meetings is usually based on factors including previous satisfaction with the service, number of changes to the service, and the likelihood of changes to the service expectations or requirements. The typical time frame is monthly but should be no longer than every three months.<br><br>No matter what the form of the review and when it takes place, service reviews are critical in the service relationship. There is a distinct relationship between the quality of a service review and the quality of the services and stakeholder satisfaction. Additionally, service reviews are the main source for service improvements – another practice PSF. |

## 5: How to align expectations and agree service details

**Table 38: PSF: Improvement Opportunities**

| PSF: Improvement opportunities |
|---|
| Service reviews provide the opportunity to improve services – based on underperformance of the service or to improve the level of satisfaction from users and customers. Of course, improvements can also be made to practices and processes, tools or other resources. Transparency is critical with improvements – ensure that any improvement suggestion is visible so that those who have made the suggestions know that they have been considered. This promotes the ITIL guiding principle of 'collaborate and promote visibility'.<br><br>All improvements to the product or service are owned by the role that is accountable (product owner or service owner). For effective implementation of practice, product and service improvements, follow the guidance in the continual improvement practice. |

# CHAPTER 6: ONBOARDING AND OFFBOARDING

This chapter is focused on step 5 of the customer journey: **onboard**.

Key topics include:

- Key transition, onboarding and offboarding activities;
- Ways of relating with users and fostering user relationships;
- How users are authorised and entitled to services;
- Approaches to mutual elevation of customer, user and service provider capabilities;
- Preparing onboarding and offboarding plans;
- Delivering user engagement and delivery channels;
- How the service catalogue management practice enables and contributes to offering user services; and
- How the service desk practice enables and contributes to user engagement.

Onboard includes the activities necessary for the service consumer to start using the service and the service provider to start delivering it. Effective onboarding enables service provision and consumption and improves the relationship between service provider and consumer.

Table 39 shows more information on the purposes of onboarding and offboarding.

## 6: Onboarding and offboarding

**Table 39: The Purposes of Onboarding and Offboarding[44]**

| Onboard and offboard | For the service consumer | For the service provider |
|---|---|---|
| Facilitate outcome and experience | To ensure a better return on investments through effective use of services<br><br>To improve user experience<br><br>To increase the effectiveness and efficiency of business operations through the effective use of services<br><br>To maximize value from cooperation with new service providers | To maximize value from cooperation with new service consumers/customers/users<br><br>To improve perception of the new services and the service provider in general<br><br>To increase customer and user loyalty and engagement |

---

[44] *ITIL® 4: Drive Stakeholder Value*, table 7.1. Copyright © AXELOS Limited 2020. Used under permission of AXELOS Limited. All rights reserved.

## 6: Onboarding and offboarding

| | | |
|---|---|---|
| Optimize risk and compliance | To decrease the probability of user incidents and questions related to new services and users<br><br>To decrease the duration of transition times to new services/providers | To decrease the probability of incidents and associated breaches in service quality<br><br>To prevent/decrease user resistance to new services and/or service providers |
| Optimize resources and minimize cost | To reduce the costs and losses associated with the transition to new services/providers<br><br>To optimize the costs of user training<br><br>To optimize the costs of user support | To reduce transition costs<br><br>To reduce user support costs<br><br>To optimize onboarding costs and overall resource utilization |

**Onboarding, offboarding and user relationships**

*Designing for onboarding*

User-centred design includes designing the onboarding approach for each product, service and service offering. The onboarding approach varies depending on the structure of

## 6: Onboarding and offboarding

service offerings, consumer resources, scale, legal and regulatory requirements, risks, etc.

### Onboarding

Onboarding includes:

- Building awareness about new or changed service consumers among all stakeholders;
- Ensuring all relevant resources are ready; and
- Ensuring customers and users are ready.

Successful onboarding requires input and involvement from both the service provider and the service consumer. Onboarding creates the first impression of a service for users, so it is important that it goes well. Onboarding occurs after an agreement is reached or changed, but before service consumption starts.

These ITIL practices support onboarding from the service provider's perspective:

- Deployment management
- Organisational change management
- Release management
- Service configuration management
- Service design
- Service desk
- Service level management

### Offboarding

Offboarding requires a similar approach to onboarding: plan and carry out activities according to the plan. Offboarding considerations need to be addressed during service design,

## 6: Onboarding and offboarding

and include data, security and asset management considerations.

Practices that support offboarding include:

- Change enablement
- Information security management
- IT asset management
- Service configuration management

Other practices will provide support where necessary, depending on the nature and scope of the service.

Offboarding activities need to be reviewed and any possible improvements to relationship management identified and actioned. If a consumer leaves because of a dispute or dissatisfaction, the reasons need to be identified. Following the offboarding plan helps to ensure the offboarding process doesn't create any further friction or bad feeling. This is especially relevant if legal action is expected.

> Onboarding and offboarding are examples of value streams where many different parts of the organisation come together. For example, think about how you were onboarded into your last new role. The activities might have involved facilities management, security, human resources, learning and development, access management, and others.

## 6: Onboarding and offboarding

> These value streams are still weak in many organisations. Poor offboarding leaves users with access to services they are no longer entitled to and can lead to wasted time and money, as well as having possible security consequences. Poor onboarding means a user isn't getting value as soon as they should, again leading to potential wasted time and money.
>
> Many IT service management tools offer the option to fully automate this type of value stream, so if this is an area of concern for your organisation, automation may be a good approach.

### *Relating with users and fostering relationships*

The amount of interaction users have with a service will vary. For example, you might access your online banking every day, but use a theatre website to order tickets once a year (or even just on a single occasion!). User experience (UX) is an important part of service satisfaction. Poor UX can lead to low user productivity and users switching to other services. UX needs to be assessed at every stage of the customer journey.

> As consumers become more and more IT literate and products and services are more commoditised, our attention spans get shorter. Think about how you use online services to engage with service providers. How

## 6: Onboarding and offboarding

> much delay will you tolerate? How quickly do you drop out of an over-complicated purchase process?
>
> As competition becomes more fierce in the digital space, service providers must have laser-like focus on UX.

### *Enabling users for service*

Some services require user skills or rights to be checked and validated, for example:

- A driving licence check before hiring a car;
- Management approval before accessing sensitive data; and
- Software training before rights are granted.

Service providers need to be able to:

- Collect requirements from relevant stakeholders;
- Apply relevant actions;
- Control implementation; and
- Continually check requirement relevance.

The user-facing service catalogue supports user enablement by showing users only relevant services and providing information in a clear and concise way.

The service desk will also support user enablement and provide different support channels (phone, app, walk-in, etc.) where necessary. The service catalogue and service desk management practices are particularly relevant in this area.

# 6: Onboarding and offboarding

## Elevating mutual capabilities

Service relationships are based on value co-creation. The table below shows how the guiding principles can be used to support service relationship success.

**Table 40: The Guiding Principles and Service Relationships[45]**

| Guiding Principle | Considerations |
|---|---|
| Focus on value | Users should understand the purpose and context of their work and of service usage. They should be encouraged to offer improvements that may contribute to value creation. |
| Start where you are | Improvement of experience should be based on current practices, habits and expectations. Radical changes in experiences are rarely seen as improvements and often resisted by users. |
| Progress iteratively with feedback | Changes in services, procedures or experience should be tested and reviewed by users. Users should be encouraged to provide feedback; follow-up should be transparent. |

---

[45] Based on *ITIL® 4: Drive Stakeholder Value*, table 7.8 "Examples of service providers and customers using the ITIL guiding principles to improve user capabilities". Copyright © AXELOS Limited 2020. Used under permission of AXELOS Limited. All rights reserved.

## 6: Onboarding and offboarding

| | |
|---|---|
| **Collaborate and promote visibility** | Users should understand need for collaboration and help each other, and the service provider, and other parties. Calling for help or reporting an incident should be safe, easy and encouraged. |
| **Think and work holistically** | Services and their role in value co-creation should be visible and transparent to all involved parties. Users should understand the context of their work and dependencies. |
| **Keep it simple and practical** | User interfaces and interactions should be as simple and friendly as possible. Users should be able to propose improvements to the interface, and these proposals should be treated seriously and transparently. |
| **Optimise and automate** | Continual optimisation and automation of user experience should be a theme of all interactions between users and service providers. |

Service consumers can support value co-creation by:

- Inviting service provider teams to observe their activities;
- Letting the service provider know about planned changes and involving them where appropriate;
- Providing feedback and contributing to user communities; and

- Forming joint teams where necessary.

## Planning onboarding and offboarding, user engagement

### *Planning onboarding*

Service design thinking is an effective way to tackle problems, drawing on engagement from real users. Service design thinking aims to *"identify solutions to the original challenge that are desirable, feasible, and viable"*. Applying service design thinking to user onboarding will create a smooth service interaction, setting the right tone for the service provider/consumer relationship. Planning onboarding is a collaborative activity between the service provider and the service consumer. If the customer isn't involved, there is more chance that they won't be ready, or that a vital activity is missed.

An onboarding plan needs to consider:

- The current status of the service relationship;
- The scope of the onboarding initiative;
- The current configuration of resources; and
- Any associated risks.

The onboarding plan needs to address these questions:

- *"What are the goals of the onboarding?*
- *What is the scope of the onboarding?*
- *What are the onboarding actions?*
- *Who is responsible for the onboarding actions?*
- *How can the onboarding be controlled and its success ensured?"*

# 6: Onboarding and offboarding

## Onboarding goals

All stakeholders need to understand the onboarding goals. Goals need to be defined, agreed and then shared. The success of onboarding should be measured in terms of outcomes achieved, not just ticking items off on a list (outputs).

The roles involved in the process may include:

- *"Product owners*
- *Service owners*
- *Account managers*
- *Relationship managers*
- *Business partners"*

The consumer is responsible for agreeing the goals and communicating them to their own stakeholders.

## Onboarding scope

The scope of onboarding can be defined by asking:

*"What are the consumer resources requiring onboarding? What are the provider resources required for onboarding? When does onboarding start and end?"*

Table 41 shows examples of consumer resources to onboard.

## 6: Onboarding and offboarding

**Table 41: Examples of Consumer Resources To Onboard**[46]

| Service management dimension | Examples of resources | Examples of the need for onboarding |
|---|---|---|
| Organizations and people | Users (employees of the consumer organization) | To enable effective use of the service, users need training in the use of the services and the support setup |
| Value streams and processes | Consumer organization procedures, actions, and workflows | Procedures should be adjusted to integrate services, technologies, and service provider people |
| Information and technology | Consumer organization technology, data, and IT services | Service provider representatives should be granted access to the consumer organization's |

---

[46] *ITIL® 4: Drive Stakeholder Value*, table 7.2. Copyright © AXELOS Limited 2020. Used under permission of AXELOS Limited. All rights reserved.

## 6: Onboarding and offboarding

|  |  |  | IT resources; IT resources should be integrated with those of the service provider; data and information should be migrated and/or converted |
|---|---|---|---|
|  | Partners and suppliers | Users (employees of the consumer organization's suppliers and partners acting as new service users) | Users (representing the consumer organization's suppliers and partners) require training in the use of services and in support procedures |

Onboarding planning needs to consider both the customer and the user perspective. Different scenarios also apply, including:

- A new consumer/user for existing services;
- A new customer/user within an existing consumer;
- An existing customer/user accessing new services; and
- A service or product, or a service consumer being migrated from another provider.

# 6: Onboarding and offboarding

Onboarding may begin at different times, depending on the onboarding scope and context. It may start, for example:

- When an agreement is reached;
- When a contract is signed;
- When services have been deployed and are ready for release;
- When services are being deployed;
- When users are formally employed within the service consumer; or
- When users have employment provisionally agreed.

The plan also needs to define when onboarding is complete.

## Onboarding actions

The ITIL principle 'keep things simple and practical' should be applied to onboarding. The activities need to be reviewed and controlled. The control approach will be agreed as part of the plan, allowing the success of the onboarding to be validated. At the end of the onboarding, it is good practice to hold a review, including:

- Formal confirmation that all actions are complete;
- A review of all stakeholders' satisfaction and experience;
- A review of any outstanding actions;
- A review of any errors, making plans for improvement by the continual improvement practice; and
- Risk assessment.

Table 42 shows examples of approaches to onboarding control.

## 6: Onboarding and offboarding

**Table 42: Examples of Approaches To Onboarding Control**[47]

| How the onboarding initiative is managed | How onboarding progress and successes are controlled and validated | ITIL practices supporting the approach | Applicability |
|---|---|---|---|
| Programme | Programme and project plans, work packages, reviews, and KPIs | Organizational change management, project management | Large customer and user onboarding initiatives requiring complex changes of various resources |
| Project | Project plans, work packages, reviews, and KPIs | Organizational change management, project management | Most of the service consumer onboarding initiatives of corporate services |

---

[47] *ITIL® 4: Drive Stakeholder Value*, table 7.5. Copyright © AXELOS Limited 2020. Used under permission of AXELOS Limited. All rights reserved.

## 6: Onboarding and offboarding

| Normal change | Custom-defined checklists | Change enablement, deployment management, organizational change management, release management, service validation and testing | Smaller service consumer onboarding initiatives, mostly where new services are introduced to existing consumers |
|---|---|---|---|
| Standard change | Pre-defined checklists | Change enablement, deployment management, organizational change management, release management, and service validation and testing | Most user onboarding initiatives of corporate services |
| Automated deployment and release (for example, plug-and-play) | Pre-installed automated tests and controls | Deployment management, infrastructure and platform management, monitoring and event management, release | Most onboarding initiatives of digital services provided to individual service consumers |

## 6: Onboarding and offboarding

|  |  | management, and software development and management | and many user onboarding initiatives of corporate services |
|---|---|---|---|
| Audits and assurance | Third-party audits, audit opinions, statements of assurance, on-site inspections, etc. | Information security management, measurement and reporting, risk management, and supplier management | Formal service relationships or relationships in highly regulated environments |

### *Planning offboarding*

Offboarding needs to be planned and managed in the same way as onboarding. This may be the customer's final memory of a product or service, so it is important to make it a positive experience. Onboarding and offboarding are a critical part of the consumer journey, so plan them carefully to ensure they meet expectations.

### *User engagement*

There are many different channels available for user interaction. Channels include social media, chatbots, chat, phone, email, self-service portal, face to face. Emerging technologies like machine learning and artificial intelligence can be applied across many of these channels to optimise support and automate resolution where possible. Be aware

## 6: Onboarding and offboarding

that not all users want to interact with a human agent, but some will prefer that option. It's important to work with your own consumers and users to try to understand their preferences.

If the UX for engagement involves multiple channels, the service provider needs to provide a seamless, 'omni-channel' experience. Corporate users will expect support to be comparable to the support they experience when using digital services at home, for example Amazon or Netflix.

Figure 22[48] shows an 'omni-channel' experience, where the customer receives a seamless experience while interacting with multiple channels.

---

[48] *ITIL® 4: Drive Stakeholder Value*, figure 7.1. Copyright © AXELOS Limited 2020. Used under permission of AXELOS Limited. All rights reserved.

*6: Onboarding and offboarding*

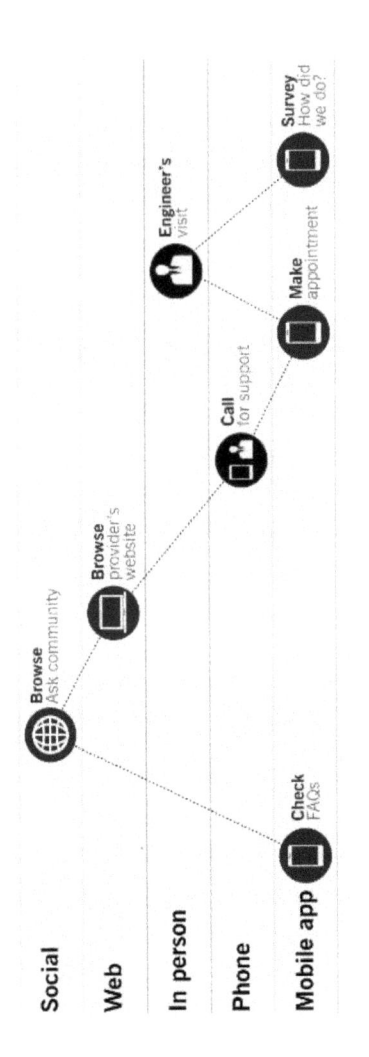

**Figure 22: Seamless user journey with omni-channel management**

## 6: Onboarding and offboarding

To deliver effective user engagement, you will need to consider areas such as:

- Stakeholders;
- Internal or external resources;
- Escalation paths and work methods: dedicated, standby, swarming, self-support, shift left*; and
- Hours and levels of support.

* Shift left in a user engagement context means moving knowledge closer to the customer to improve resolution times and customer experience. This could be via FAQs and self-service portals, via better trained front-line teams, or using approaches like swarming. Swarming takes a different approach to traditional tiered support systems by allocating work to the resource(s) most likely to resolve it. It takes a more dynamic approach to resolving issues.

Table 43 shows some of the challenges associated with omni-channel management.

**Table 43: Examples of Omni-channel Challenges That Have To Be Considered By Service Providers[49]**

| Approach | Example challenges | Example solutions |
|---|---|---|
| *Shift-left, increase of self-service* | *Users do not have sufficient technology* | *Train support agents in social media communications* |

---

[49] *ITIL® 4: Drive Stakeholder Value*, table 7.7. Copyright © AXELOS Limited 2020. Used under permission of AXELOS Limited. All rights reserved.

## 6: Onboarding and offboarding

| Approach | Example challenges | Example solutions |
|---|---|---|
|  | skills and/or motivation to use the self-service tools<br><br>Only a limited range of tasks can be fulfilled by users at their level of access to the service<br><br>Mistakes made by users during self-service may cause more incidents<br><br>Knowledge-based navigation may be difficult | Automate the monitoring of user testimonies using hashtags and other mentions of the service/service provider<br><br>Integrate social media channels with specialized support systems. Keep records and handle sensitive information in those systems<br><br>Ensure all calls for support in social media are promptly responded to and handled to the users' satisfaction |
| Social media support | An emotional and difficult-to-control style of communication<br><br>Viral effect, high exposure to mistakes and conflicts | Train support agents in social media communications<br><br>Automate the monitoring of user testimonies using hashtags and other mentions of the |

## 6: Onboarding and offboarding

| Approach | Example challenges | Example solutions |
|---|---|---|
|  | Unstructured information | service/service provider |
|  | Multiple channels to monitor and reply to | Integrate social media channels with specialized support systems. Keep records and handle sensitive information in those systems |
|  | Constraints in handling personal and contractual information |  |
|  | No integrated diagnostic tools | Ensure all calls for support in social media are promptly responded to and handled to the users' satisfaction |
|  | No formal records system under service provider's control |  |
| *Familiar interfaces* | Legacy systems used by a service provider may limit the compatibility and interface design | Design products and services for continual development and flexibility, minimize use of monolithic and legacy products |
|  | Commonly used applications and operating systems evolve, and usually multiple | Consider offering interfaces adapted for users of different platforms |
|  |  | When offering custom interfaces, design for |

## 6: Onboarding and offboarding

| Approach | Example challenges | Example solutions |
|---|---|---|
| | platforms and versions co-exist<br><br>Some services require specialized equipment and interfaces | usability and, where possible, follow the use patterns of commonly used services and interfaces |
| *Machine learning: chatbots* | Limited applicability<br><br>Insufficient and inadequate data for machine learning<br><br>Difficulties of multi-language support | Do not replace human interfaces with machine-learning based until level of success is high enough; provide human back-up<br><br>Expand the scope of machine-learning based service interactions iteratively, include multiple feedback loops<br><br>Continually increase the quality of data in all languages used for service interactions with users |

## 6: Onboarding and offboarding

| Approach | Example challenges | Example solutions |
|---|---|---|
| **Machine learning: optimized delivery channels** | Limited applicability<br><br>Insufficient and inadequate data for machine learning<br><br>Changes in both user's behaviour and support organization<br><br>Limited resources | Monitor and exploit developments in machine learning<br><br>Focus on the most important and popular patterns of support<br><br>Ensure high quality of support history data Optimize, then automate<br><br>Back up new technology solutions with experienced support agents |
| **Human support agents** | Limited scalability<br><br>Probability of mistakes<br><br>Emotional attitude<br><br>High cost | Support agents' motivation, retention, and professional development<br><br>Limit human support to situations where it is needed and justified<br><br>Consider peer-to-peer support to |

## 6: Onboarding and offboarding

| Approach | Example challenges | Example solutions |
|---|---|---|
| | | *increase scalability and optimize costs* |
| *Video diagnostic* | *Use of users' devices may be limited by technical, legal, and regulatory constraints*<br><br>*Privacy concerns*<br><br>*Use of data for video may incur extra costs to user* | *Warn users about possible risks and costs*<br><br>*Ensure applicable regulations are met*<br><br>*Implement controls to prevent the abuse of the technology* |
| *Enhanced monitoring* | *Technology and privacy constraints, especially when services are provided using service consumer's infrastructure* | *Discuss benefits, risks, and costs with customers, consider discussing them with users*<br><br>*Make sure applicable regulations are met*<br><br>*Implement controls to prevent the abuse of the technology* |

To deliver a good omni-channel experience, the service provider needs to allocate enough resources: financial,

*6: Onboarding and offboarding*

technical and organisational. The service provider must be able to:

- Identify a user across all channels;
- Access relevant user data across all channels; and
- Monitor and manage the user journey across all channels.

**The service catalogue management practice**

The service catalogue management practice provides a single, consistent source of information about services and service offerings to all stakeholders. The practice purpose is:

*"To provide a single source of consistent information on all services and service offerings, and to ensure that it is available to the relevant audience."*

A service catalogue provides *"structured information about all the services and service offerings of a service provider, relevant for a specific target audience"*.

The service catalogue offers different information to different stakeholders, depending on their needs and level of access. Different internal and external stakeholders may be able to view the service catalogue, including users, current and potential customers, product teams, support teams, supplier managers, relationship managers, etc.

The service catalogue management practice works closely with other practices including:

- Service configuration management
- Service financial management
- Relationship management
- Service request management

## 6: Onboarding and offboarding

- Supplier management

The service catalogue includes the internal and external services managed by an organisation, as well as the services provided and consumed. For example, the supplier manager role may be able to see information about external services consumed by the organisation that support the organisation's own services.

### *Practice success factors*

There are two practice success factors (PSFs) for service catalogue management. The PSFs are:

- *"Ensuring that the organization's service catalogues' structure and scope meet organizational requirements*
- *Ensuring that the information in service catalogues meets stakeholders' current and anticipated needs."*

**Table 44: PSF: Aligning Service Catalogue Structure and Scope To Organisational Requirements**

| PSF: Aligning service catalogue structure and scope to organisational requirements |
|---|
| The service catalogue's structure and scope should reflect the organisation's business, product and service architectures. The service catalogue management practice will use inputs from strategy management, architecture management and portfolio management to help deliver this. |
| The service catalogue design will be subject to continual improvement. Improvements may be identified via: <br> • Reviews; |

## 6: Onboarding and offboarding

- User feedback;
- Requirement changes;
- Changes to the organisation's architecture; and
- Technology changes or opportunities.

**Table 45: PSF: Ensuring Information Meets Current and Future Stakeholder Needs**

| PSF: Ensuring information meets current and future stakeholder needs |
|---|
| Service catalogue maintenance, updates and provision should be automated as much as possible. Tailored views are agreed and created. |
| The ability to create multiple views from one service catalogue is more efficient than hosting and maintaining multiple catalogues, although this may be necessary in some situations. Service catalogue usage needs to be monitored and measured to identify any errors and track stakeholder satisfaction levels. The practice will promote the service catalogue and encourage its use by all relevant stakeholders. |
| The service catalogue is one of the key interfaces between service providers and service consumers, so it should be easy to use to support widespread adoption. Service catalogue design needs to consider how to make the service catalogue smooth, intuitive and simple. A poor service catalogue experience can inhibit service take-up and damage the service provider/consumer relationship. |

## 6: Onboarding and offboarding

Table 46 provides more information about different service catalogue views:

**Table 46: Service Catalogue Views**

| | |
|---|---|
| **User view** | Provides information about services and service offerings from the user's perspective. The user should only see the services they are entitled to request or access. This view may include:<br>• Service description<br>• How to request the service<br>• SLAs<br>• Technical and support information<br>• Prerequisites and authorisation |
| **Customer view** | This view contains business information including service levels, financial data, service performance and measurements, etc. The view will be further tailored depending on whether the customer is a potential, new or existing customer. |
| **Service provider view** | This view of the catalogue shows service delivery information including:<br>• Technical<br>• Security<br>• Risk<br>• Process<br><br>Different service provider teams may see different information; for example, a |

## 6: Onboarding and offboarding

> service desk analyst and a business analyst will need different levels of data.

### The service desk practice

Most of us have experienced an interaction with a service desk and we come away from that engagement with a positive or negative impression of the organisation behind it. The service desk is often the first and only encounter we have with a service-providing organisation, and it is sometimes described as the 'shop window'. The service desk needs to deliver a great user experience and work to achieve high levels of customer satisfaction.

The purpose of the service desk is *"to capture demand for incident resolution and service requests. It should also be the entry point and single point of contact for the service provider for all users."*

An incident is *"an unplanned interruption to a service or reduction in the quality of a service".*

The service desk team typically supports multiple service management practices including:

- Incident management
- Service request management
- Problem management
- Service configuration management
- Relationship management practices

These relationships are based on the direct contact and communication the service desk has with users. Any value stream activity that requires user communication will use the service desk.

# 6: Onboarding and offboarding

## Communication channels

The service desk practice establishes effective and convenient communication channels between users and the service provider. This can include multiple channels delivering a seamless experience (omni-channel).

## Service empathy

A critical characteristic of a service desk role is the ability to empathise. Service empathy is *"the ability to recognize, understand, predict, and project the interests, needs, intentions, and experiences of another party in order to establish, maintain, and improve the service relationship"*.

Service empathy is a critical element of user satisfaction and the success of the service provider. Service empathy is usually fulfilled via human, not automated, interactions.

## User satisfaction

User satisfaction is heavily influenced by interactions with the service desk.

Service providers need to monitor 'moments of truth'. A moment of truth is *"any episode in which the customer or user comes into contact with an aspect of the organization and gets an impression of the quality of its service. It is the basis for setting and fulfilling client expectations and ultimately achieving client satisfaction."*

The service desk practice can be a channel for collecting information about user satisfaction. Remember that users will only engage with surveys and measures if they feel their response will be treated seriously and fairly, with action taken where needed.

## 6: Onboarding and offboarding

***Practice success factors***

The service desk practice includes two practice success factors:

*"Enabling and continually improving effective, efficient, and convenient communications between the service provider and its users.*

*Enabling the effective integration of user communications into value streams."*

**Table 47: PSF: Enabling and Improving Communications Between The Service Provider and Its Users**

| PSF: Enabling and improving communications between the service provider and its users |
|---|
| Support channels for users should be easy to locate, be easy to use, and provide all necessary support efficiently. The design of the user interface is determined by numerous factors such as:<br><br>• Service relationship model and type – is the relationship public or private, internal or external; is the type of relationship basic, cooperative, or a partnership?<br>• User profile – what are their capabilities based on location, age, culture, diversity, etc.?<br>• Service provider profile – what are their technical capabilities, user satisfaction strategy, etc.?<br>• External factors – consider PESTLE impacts.<br><br>Due to the advances in technology, communication channels for user support can be provided by a human or |

## 6: Onboarding and offboarding

through technology. Some examples of communication channels include:

- Voice
- Live chat
- Email
- Walk-in
- Web portals
- Interactive voice menus
- Mobile applications
- Chatbots

Table 48 shows examples of channels and the challenges associated with them.

**Table 48: Examples of Channels and Their Challenges**[50]

| Channel | Example challenges | Example solutions |
|---|---|---|
| Voice | Limited scalability<br><br>Subjective attitudes and emotions | Limit human support to where it is needed and justified<br><br>Invest in support agents' professional |

---

[50] *ITIL® 4: Service Desk Practice Guide*, table 2.4. Copyright © AXELOS Limited 2020. Used under permission of AXELOS Limited. All rights reserved.

## 6: Onboarding and offboarding

| | Channel | Example challenges | Example solutions |
|---|---|---|---|
| | | | development, emotional intelligence, awareness of diverse cultures, and interests |
| User-to-human interactions | Live-chat | Subjective attitudes and emotions | Limit human support to where it is needed and justified |
| | Email | Unstructured information Subjective attitudes and emotions | Leverage available resources to automate the logging of unstructured information, where appropriate |
| | Walk-In | Limited scalability Subjective attitudes and emotions | Promote self-service where appropriate to increase adoption |

## 6: Onboarding and offboarding

|  | Channel | Example challenges | Example solutions |
|---|---|---|---|
| | Concierge | Limited scope and availability<br><br>Subjective attitudes and emotions | Promote self-service where appropriate to increase adoption |
| | Social media | Viral effect, high exposure of mistakes and conflicts<br><br>Subjective attitudes and emotions<br><br>Unstructured information<br><br>Security constraints | Provide clear security parameters and regularly test their effectiveness |
| User-to-technology interactions | Web portals, interactive voice (phone) menus, mobile applications, chat-bots, and so on | Limited range of tasks can be fulfilled by users at their security level<br><br>Insufficient and | Assess user skills and available range of support actions before implementing self-help<br><br>Use channels and interfaces |

## 6: Onboarding and offboarding

| Channel | Example challenges | Example solutions |
|---|---|---|
| | inadequate data | familiar to users |
| | Insufficient and inadequate user technology skills | Ensure a high quality of support history data and knowledge |
| | Lack of service empathy and emotional intelligence | When using machine learning, ensure a high quality of data and algorithms |
| | Limited applicability to complicated and complex situations | Provide human back-up support options |
| | | Improve information quality and navigation tools |
| | | Ensure self-help tools and actions are as accessible as possible |

Typically, service providers will use multiple channels to provide user support. These channels should be connected

## 6: Onboarding and offboarding

and integrated or omni-channel, allowing the user to start a support call using a mobile application to create an appointment, follow up with a call to a service desk, and eventually have a solution applied by a technician without having to repeatedly provide information. Multichannel communication that is not well integrated could require information to be re-entered at each step, with a risk of creating gaps in the support actions or losing or corrupting information.

**Table 49: PSF: Integrating Communication Into Value Streams**

| PSF: Integrating communication into value streams |
|---|
| The service desk provides bi-directional communication between the service provider and the user. The service desk practice focuses on the accuracy of capturing, recording and integrating communication into relevant value streams. |
| One example of a communication by the service provider to the user would be a notification around planned changes. The content, format and timing of the message is determined by change enablement and release management practices, but the service desk establishes and maintains the communication channel. |
| User-initiated communication (queries) must be triaged* by the service desk, so it is forwarded to the appropriate value stream. Once forwarded, that specific value stream processes and acts upon the query following each value stream's specific processes and procedures. |

## 6: Onboarding and offboarding

*The concept of triage comes from a military medical context. It focuses on identifying the most urgent work so it can be dealt with first. Low-priority work has to wait until high- and medium-priority work has been completed. Triage can be used to manage workloads such as development backlogs and incident queues. It's important to make sure the low-priority work doesn't get left forever though.

> One of Banksbest's strategic goals is to build a reputation as a digital-first banking provider. How do you think that might affect its service desk practice and the type of channels it offers for support? What type of support could reinforce this concept of 'digital first'?

# CHAPTER 7: CONTINUAL VALUE CO-CREATION

This chapter is focused on step 6 of the customer journey: **co-create**.

The key concepts include:

- How users can request services;
- Methods for triaging user requests;
- The concept of user communities;
- How to encourage and manage customer and user feedback;
- How to foster a service mindset;
- How to use different approaches to provisioning user services;
- How to seize and deal with customer and user moments of truth; and
- How the service request management practice can be applied to enable and contribute to service usage.

All of the customer journey so far has been preparation for this step, where value will be delivered. This service provision and consumption step includes:

- Service delivery and support
- Service consumption
- Service usage

## 7: Continual value co-creation

Table 50 shows more information on the purpose of service provision and consumption.

**Table 50: The Purpose of Service Provision and Consumption**[51]

| Co-create | For the service consumer | For the service provider |
|---|---|---|
| Facilitate outcome and experience | To maximize actual outcomes from the service consumption and service relationship<br><br>To improve user and customer functional experience through correct consumption<br><br>To improve users' and customers' emotional experiences through effective collaboration<br><br>To improve external | To improve customers' and users' loyalty<br><br>To maximize outcomes from service provision and service relationships<br><br>To obtain valuable input for continual improvement through feedback and moments of truth<br><br>To improve employees' satisfaction<br><br>To increase productivity |

---

[51] *ITIL® 4: Drive Stakeholder Value*, table 8.1. Copyright © AXELOS Limited 2020. Used under permission of AXELOS Limited. All rights reserved.

## 7: Continual value co-creation

| Co-create | For the service consumer | For the service provider |
|---|---|---|
| | stakeholder satisfaction<br><br>To improve employees' satisfaction<br><br>To increase productivity | |
| Optimize risk and compliance | To decrease the risk of value leakages through better alignment and realistic expectations<br><br>To decrease the risk of recurring deviations of service quality through responsive support and the value-oriented prioritization of service improvements<br><br>To decrease the risk of information losses through effective | To decrease the probability of incidents and associated breaches in service quality<br><br>To increase users' tolerance to service quality deviations through loyalty 'credit' |

## 7: Continual value co-creation

| Co-create | For the service consumer | For the service provider |
|---|---|---|
| | communications and collaboration | |
| Optimize resources and minimize cost | To reduce losses associated with poor quality of the services being consumed<br><br>To optimize the costs of service consumption | To optimize the operational costs of service provision<br><br>To reduce the user support costs |

**Fostering a service mindset**

Key considerations related to a service mindset include:

- Service mindset for service provision;
- Intelligent disobedience;
- Services with invisible users;
- Service mindset for service consumption; and
- How to seize and deal with moments of truth.

*Service mindset for service provision*

*"Service empathy is the ability to recognize, understand, predict, and project the interests, needs, intentions, and experiences of another party in order to establish, maintain, and improve the service relationship."*

Service empathy is a concept that applies outside the scope of user support. Service providers and consumers need to

# 7: Continual value co-creation

work together, acting responsibly and focusing on agreed outcomes. Service empathy is an important skill for anyone working in service management. The closer the relationship, the more empathy is required. A service mindset includes service empathy, as well as these values and principles:

- Know your customer/user and their expectations.
- Focus on value, and take responsibility.
- Acknowledge and adapt to culture.
- Encourage collaboration and show generosity.
- Show ingenuity, including intelligent disobedience.
- Behave ethically at all times.

## Intelligent disobedience

Intelligent disobedience is *"deliberately disobeying or disregarding rules in order to avoid a dangerous situation, or 'doing the right thing'"*.

In essence, staff are able to break the rules to do the right thing. It's very important that staff understand how far intelligent disobedience can go in their organisation and feel safe and empowered when they 'disobey'. For intelligent disobedience to work in an organisation, service providers should:

- Recognise that rules or procedures in place are not appropriate for every single situation;
- Encourage and empower their staff to help them understand and fulfil unmet requirements;
- Create a safe environment for staff; and
- Document any actions and identify where improvements could be made.

# 7: Continual value co-creation

ITIL's guiding principles should guide professional behaviour for service provider staff. Table 51 shows examples for all the ITIL guiding principles.

**Table 51: Service Mindset In A Service Provider Organization[52]**

| ITIL guiding principle | Key questions | Examples of learning and development methods |
|---|---|---|
| Focus on value | *Who are the potential customers?* *How do they perceive value from the services? What kind of experience do the customers expect?* *How can everyone involved contribute to value co-creation?* | *Introduction to the service consumer's business (where applicable, a visit to the service consumer's premises)* *Introduction to the user support (where applicable, participation in user support)* *Introduction to the service architecture and dependencies* |

---

[52] *ITIL® 4: Drive Stakeholder Value*, table 8.2. Copyright © AXELOS Limited 2020. Used under permission of AXELOS Limited. All rights reserved.

## 7: Continual value co-creation

| ITIL guiding principle | Key questions | Examples of learning and development methods |
|---|---|---|
| Start where you are | What is the service consumer's context and history? What is the service consumer's previous use of products and services? What legacy products or relationships do the service consumers have? Do the users have any special needs or expectations? How were their needs addressed before? | History and context as part of the customer onboarding and of new employees' induction Introduction to the service architecture and dependencies Where applicable, inclusivity and special needs awareness training |
| Progress iteratively with feedback | What are the moments of truth and other touchpoints and service interactions between users and | Training in feedback collection and processing Awareness and practical training in |

## 7: Continual value co-creation

| ITIL guiding principle | Key questions | Examples of learning and development methods |
|---|---|---|
| | *the service provider?* *What are the user service actions?* *How can feedback be collected about each of them?* *When feedback is provided, what are the procedures for addressing it?* *How can feedback be incorporated into continual improvement and other areas?* | *improvement initiation* *Training in processing negative feedback and effective communication techniques* |
| *Collaborate and promote visibility* | *Where is the band of visibility in the service relationship with the service consumer? What do we do together?* *Who will accept the responsible and* | *Where applicable, joint training and other activities with users and/or customers* *Introduction to the service architecture and dependencies* |

## 7: Continual value co-creation

| ITIL guiding principle | Key questions | Examples of learning and development methods |
|---|---|---|
| | accountable roles in joint activities? How are joint and visible activities visualized? What tools need to be used to demonstrate progress? What indicators are visible to the customers and users? Which indicators do they need to see? Which decisions and actions should involve users and/or customers? What is the cultural context of the service relationship? | Introduction to reporting systems, analysis of service consumer-facing reports, and mapping of the results to the employee's area of responsibility |
| Think and work holistically | How do the services contribute to the service consumer's | Introduction to the service architecture and dependencies |

## 7: Continual value co-creation

| ITIL guiding principle | Key questions | Examples of learning and development methods |
|---|---|---|
| | activities and objectives?<br><br>Which teams in our organization are involved in the service relationship?<br><br>Which partners and supplier relationships are involved?<br><br>How does information flow in various value streams? How can information be exchanged with the service consumer, partners, and suppliers? | Introduction to the service consumer's business (where applicable, a visit to the service consumer's premises)<br><br>Introduction to reporting systems, analysis of service consumer-facing reports, and mapping of the results to the employee's area of responsibility |
| Keep it simple and practical | What interfaces are available to users and customers?<br><br>What does the user journey look like? | Take the user journey<br><br>Training in the service architecture |

## 7: Continual value co-creation

| ITIL guiding principle | Key questions | Examples of learning and development methods |
|---|---|---|
| | *How satisfied are users and customers with service interactions?*<br><br>*How will each decision influence user experience?*<br><br>*If there is an experience improvement opportunity, how it can be realized?* | *Where applicable, simplified user training for service provider's teams*<br><br>*Awareness/training in the organization's continual improvement practice* |
| *Optimize and automate* | *What service actions can be performed as part of service provision and consumption?*<br><br>*Are there service actions that can be optimized?*<br><br>*Are there manual service actions which could be automated?* | *Where applicable, simplified user training for service provider's teams*<br><br>*Introduction to the service architecture and dependencies*<br><br>*Awareness/training in the organization's continual* |

## 7: Continual value co-creation

| ITIL guiding principle | Key questions | Examples of learning and development methods |
|---|---|---|
|  | *How can improvement opportunities be realized?* | *improvement practice* |

Deliberately breaking the rules is a frightening idea for many people. But think about the value from both a customer and a provider perspective.

For the customer, intelligent disobedience can lead to a better overall experience. You might have experienced frustration yourself when dealing with a service desk. You may have found yourself, like me, on occasion thinking "they are just following a script!" Giving support staff room to think outside the box allows them to have a much more human relationship with the customer and that will lead to a better customer experience.

From the provider's perspective, staff have more autonomy and empowerment. They can take ownership of and interest in a problem, leading to innovative solutions that go far beyond scripted answers.

## 7: Continual value co-creation

> For this to work, staff must feel safe and know they will not be punished for going against normal procedures.
>
> Based on my own experiences, there is also a flip side to think about here. Standard responses have been standardised for a reason: to provide a common approach to a repeated problem or question. If we 'train' our customers to think they will get a different answer if they complain enough, or get through to the right person, we'll make our support environment much more challenging. For example, we might have excess fees for going above a certain level of usage. Applying these allows us to cover our costs and helps to shape consumer demand. We don't want every single customer to ring and challenge their late fees in the hope of getting a refund because they know some staff will do this to make them happy. There will always be an imbalance in the customer/service provider relationship when every customer believes they have a unique situation, but the service provider is seeing the same thing over and over again. From a customer experience perspective, it's a real challenge!

### *Services with invisible users*

Some organisations offer services without direct users, such as platform or infrastructure services. For example, an office cleaner working outside office hours might never interact with people in the office they are cleaning. This can lead to the service provider losing focus on their end users. Instead, it might focus on technology, or equipment.

### *Service mindset for service consumption*

Service consumers also need to have a service mindset. Without this, value co-creation cannot take place. Again, this

## 7: Continual value co-creation

is guided by the ITIL guiding principles. For example, 'focus on value' includes knowing what the service is being used for, and what your expectations as a consumer are.

Table 52 shows examples for all the ITIL guiding principles.

**Table 52: Service Mindset In A Service Consumer Organization**[53]

| ITIL guiding principle | Key questions | Examples of learning and development methods |
|---|---|---|
| Focus on value | What is the service being used for? What are the expected outcomes and value? What service experience is expected? What else contributes to the expected outcomes? How does the service interact with other services and the organization's resources? | Awareness training: introducing everyone to the operating model, key value streams, and role of the services in the organization |

---

[53] *ITIL® 4: Drive Stakeholder Value*, table 8.3. Copyright © AXELOS Limited 2020. Used under permission of AXELOS Limited. All rights reserved.

## 7: Continual value co-creation

| ITIL guiding principle | Key questions | Examples of learning and development methods |
|---|---|---|
|  | Are there contradictory stakeholder requirements? How good is the customer (or the service provider) at representing their area of interest? |  |
| **Start where you are** | Are there other ways to achieve the outcomes? Are they proven and effective? What should be retained from the current and previous practices and relationships when the service is being developed/improved? | Regular cross-team meetings to synchronize and maintain a shared understanding of the current state and its context Knowledge management, including access to information about the organization's practices and lessons |

## 7: Continual value co-creation

| ITIL guiding principle | Key questions | Examples of learning and development methods |
|---|---|---|
| **Progress iteratively with feedback** | How can feedback to the service provider be provided?<br><br>How can feedback to the service provider and other stakeholders be received?<br><br>How can feedback be processed to ensure progress? | Online and offline information about available feedback channels<br><br>Regular meetings of the key users and customers with service providers<br><br>Joint activities such as testing and training, especially when services are being changed<br><br>Awareness training and visual information about |
| **Collaborate and promote visibility** | What are the users' and customers' responsibilities during service consumption? | Practical and up-to-date knowledge base for users, including visual aids, joint |

## 7: Continual value co-creation

| ITIL guiding principle | Key questions | Examples of learning and development methods |
|---|---|---|
|  | Are the requirements being met? Are the agreed rules of service consumption being followed?<br><br>Where is the band of visibility in the service relationship with the service provider?<br><br>How is involvement in the joint activities with the service provider going to work?<br><br>How are joint and visible activities visualized? What tools need to be used to demonstrate progress (such as Kanban boards)?<br><br>Which decisions and actions should involve the service provider? | training, and rehearsal for critical service actions<br><br>Joint training in service empathy/rapport<br><br>Introduction to work visualization tools such as Kanban<br><br>Awareness (through training, visual materials, and a knowledge base) of the support channels and available support options<br><br>Clarify who to contact in different situations and be available when the service |

## 7: Continual value co-creation

| ITIL guiding principle | Key questions | Examples of learning and development methods |
|---|---|---|
| | | *provider needs a counterpart* |
| **Think and work holistically** | *What is the context of service consumption, and how does it contribute to the objectives of the organization and to the service consumers' business?*<br><br>*How is consumption of the service integrated into the value streams?*<br><br>*How can the role of the service be improved/optimized to increase its value?*<br><br>*What dependencies and relations should be considered when consuming the service?* | *Awareness training: introducing everyone to the operating model, key value streams, and role of the services in the organization*<br><br>*Introduction and explanation of the organizational changes affecting the service architecture and relationships* |

## 7: Continual value co-creation

| ITIL guiding principle | Key questions | Examples of learning and development methods |
|---|---|---|
| **Keep it simple and practical** | What are the best ways to use the service?<br><br>If there is an experience improvement opportunity, how can it be initiated? | Awareness (through training, visual materials, knowledge base) of the use and support channels and available options |
| **Optimize and automate** | What service actions can be performed as part of service consumption?<br><br>Are there service actions that can be optimized?<br><br>Are there manual service actions which could be automated?<br><br>If there is an improvement opportunity, how can it be initiated? | Awareness training and visual information about the organization's continual improvement practice<br><br>Incentive programmes for continual improvement, focused on the value of improvement initiatives |

# 7: Continual value co-creation

## *Moments of truth*

A moment of truth is *"any episode in which the customer or user comes into contact with an aspect of the organization and gets an impression of the quality of its service. It is the basis for setting and fulfilling client expectations and ultimately achieving client satisfaction."*

Moments of truth can happen during both positive and negative events; they can make or break the service experience. The service provider needs to be aware of moments of truth and try to turn negative moments into positive ones.

## Service request and provision

Key concepts related to service request and provision include:

- Ongoing service interactions
- Service requests
- Service desk interactions
- What to do when things go wrong
- Customer and user feedback
- User communities

## *Ongoing service interactions*

Services can be provided to users in different ways.

## 7: Continual value co-creation

**Table 53: Types of Service Provision**

| | |
|---|---|
| **Push or pull** | Services and service interactions can be initiated by users ('pull') or initiated by the service provider ('push). |
| **Automated or manual** | This includes:<br><br>**Technology-free:** there is no technology involved in the service provision.<br><br>**Technology-assisted:** the service provider is supported by technology, for example the service desk uses a tool to manage requests from users.<br><br>**Technology-facilitated:** the service provider and the user have access to technology as part of service provision; for example, the service desk uses remote access software to take over the user's PC.<br><br>**Technology-mediated:** the service provider and the user aren't in physical proximity; for example, communicating via a chat function.<br><br>**Technology-generated:** the service provider, consumer, or both, are represented entirely by technology; for example, self-service. |

## 7: Continual value co-creation

| Tailored or out-of-the-box | This includes the level of standardisation and/or customisation that is possible for the interactions between users and service providers. |
|---|---|
| Direct or indirect | This describes whether the service provider uses its own resources to interact with users, or whether it uses agents. |

The service provision approach is agreed during service design. Service interactions can include:

- Joint activities where the user and service provider have a role to play;
- Service provision activities where the service provider makes goods and resources available; and
- Service consumption activities where the consumer accesses and uses goods and services.

The ongoing management and improvement of these activities will be an important part of the service provider/consumer relationship.

### Service requests

A service request is *"a request from a user or a user's authorized representative that initiates a service action which has been agreed as part of normal service delivery"*.

Fulfilling service requests is an important part of value co-creation. Service requests can include users requesting access to services, users requesting updates or maintenance to services, or users requesting a change to an existing access level.

## 7: Continual value co-creation

Service request management is supported by these ITIL practices:

- Change enablement
- IT asset management
- Service catalogue management
- Service configuration management
- Service desk
- Service level management
- Service request management

Other ITIL practices will be involved where necessary.

### *Service desk interactions*

The service desk practice *"captures demand for incident resolution and service requests. It should also be the entry point and single point of contact for the service provider for all of its users."*

For the service desk to work effectively, users must understand interfaces, procedures and rules. These are communicated during onboarding. The service desk is then continually improved based on feedback and performance measures. Users need to understand how the service desk will respond to their queries, so their expectations are set correctly. Timescales will depend on factors including:

- Type of query
- Channel used to report query
- Impact
- Level of service
- Any other factors

# 7: Continual value co-creation

Table 54 shows the ITIL practices that are involved with service desk triage.

**Table 54: User Queries: Triage Criteria and Key Practices Involved In Their Processing**[54]

| Triaging criteria | Service query type | Key ITIL practices involved |
|---|---|---|
| **Agreed SLAs are breached or user reports a negative experience** | Incidents | Incident management |
| **Agreed conditions for an emergency situation are met or the query can be linked to an ongoing registered disaster** | Disasters | Service continuity management |
| **Valid service request option is selected from the service request catalogue** | Service requests | Service request management |

---

[54] *ITIL® 4: Drive Stakeholder Value*, table 8.4. Copyright © AXELOS Limited 2020. Used under permission of AXELOS Limited. All rights reserved.

## 7: Continual value co-creation

| | | |
|---|---|---|
| **Valid change option is selected from service catalogue which is available to the user** | Change requests | Change enablement |
| **User reports negative experience that is known as not breaching any agreed SLA (complaint) or user reports a positive experience for the record** | Complaints and compliments | Relationship management |
| **User proposes improvements that are not covered by available options of service catalogue (including service request catalogue)** | Improvement proposals | Continual improvement |
| **User reports suspicious activities or events that may indicate threats to information security** | Suspicious activities and events | Information security management |

## 7: Continual value co-creation

**When things go wrong**

No service is perfect, so service providers need to be prepared to manage incidents and complaints. A service outage doesn't necessarily lead to unhappy users if it is managed correctly and users receive good communication. The service mindset and service empathy are important when things go wrong.

Service providers can use the ITIL guiding principles to help them manage incident and complaints, including:

- *"Focus on value and quick restoration of value co-creation*
- *Collect and provide feedback*
- *Communicate with the affected users transparently and honestly*
- *Demonstrate understanding and empathy*
- *Keep interactions and advice simple and practical*
- *Exercise intelligent disobedience where appropriate"*

These ITIL practices enable incident and complaint management:

- Continual improvement
- Incident management
- Knowledge management
- Relationship management
- Service desk
- Service request management

# 7: Continual value co-creation

## Customer and user feedback

Customer and user feedback supports continual improvement of services and the service provider/consumer relationship. Service providers need to gather and process feedback and demonstrate that they are taking action based on customer and user comments. This will encourage customers and users to provide honest and open feedback in the future.

> **?**
>
> Do you know how your organisation collects customer and user feedback? How often is it done, and what methods are used? What happens to the feedback once it has been collected?

## Nurturing user communities

User communities can be deliberately created and managed by the service provider or may form naturally through user-to-user interactions. They might include users from the same organisation or span multiple organisations. User communities enable peer support, knowledge sharing, discussion and improvement initiatives.

Service providers should encourage and engage with user communities. The peer support element can reduce the amount of support work the service provider needs to do, and the improvement initiatives are an important source of

# 7: Continual value co-creation

feedback. Service providers with a very diverse user group may have multiple user communities to engage with.

User communities can be enabled by ITIL practices including:

- Incident management
- Knowledge management
- Problem management
- Relationship management
- Service catalogue management
- Service desk
- Service request management
- Service validation and testing

## *Super users*

Many communities and groups track member contributions and allocate 'status' to them. In groups managed by service providers, super user roles may be created. Super users can also exist in corporate environments. A super user will have in-depth knowledge of a product or service and may have higher access rights granted to allow them to offer peer support.

Super users are often voluntary roles, motivated by a desire to help, or be part of a community, or learn more about a product or service. The role is vulnerable to staff changes, so service providers need to plan for a super user being unavailable. Service providers will sometimes create super user groups who gather to share knowledge and experiences.

# 7: Continual value co-creation

> **?**
>
> At Banksbest, Doug Range has held a super user role. What are the advantages of having business staff members trained up to an advanced level on IT services? Does it create any risks?

## The service request management practice

The service request management practice purpose is:

*"to support the agreed quality of a service by handling all predefined, user-initiated service requests in an effective and user-friendly manner".*

A service request is *"a request from a user or user's authorized representative that initiates a service action which has been agreed as a normal part of service delivery".*

Service request management forms an important part of the overall user experience. Service requests include:

- Request initiating a service action;
- Request for information;
- Request for access to a resource or service; and
- Feedback, compliments or complaints.

Service requests can normally be fulfilled by following defined procedures; these might be standard changes. Standard changes are preapproved changes with a clear workflow. They do not require individual authorisation via the change enablement practice.

## 7: Continual value co-creation

Request management and fulfilment procedures need to be developed, tested and reviewed for improvements. Service requests may need authorisation (for example financial, information security, etc.). To be effective, the practice should:

- Automate and standardise as many activities as possible;
- Establish policies around what authorisation is needed and when;
- Set user expectations based on the service provider's capabilities;
- Identify and implement improvements; and
- Identify and escalate any requests that should be handled via the change enablement or incident management practices.

Self-service options can allow service request fulfilment to be completely automated.

### *Practice success factors*

There are two practice success factors (PSFs) for service request management. The PSFs are:

*"Ensuring that the service request fulfilment procedures for all services are optimised.*

*Ensuring that all service requests are fulfilled according to the agreed procedures and to user satisfaction."*

# 7: Continual value co-creation

**Table 55: PSF: Ensuring That Service Request Fulfilment Procedures Are Optimised**

| PSF: Ensuring that service request fulfilment procedures are optimised |
|---|
| Service requests and their associated procedures should be considered during service design. What will be needed? How will requests be managed?<br><br>Some services will only have a few, very simple, request options. Others may be much more complex. Procedures need to be identified, documented and tested. Clear roles and responsibilities should be assigned and communicated.<br><br>Service request fulfilment procedures will be subject to continual improvement once they are live. Metrics such as number of requests fulfilled, time to fulfil, etc. are considered along with user satisfaction. Automation of request procedures and request models is one way to optimise their fulfilment, but should only be applied to suitable procedures. High-risk or complex procedures may not be suitable for automation. |

**Table 56: PSF: Ensuring That Requests Are Fulfilled Appropriately**

| PSF: Ensuring that requests are fulfilled appropriately |
|---|
| Service request fulfilment should be easy to track if procedures are clear and well documented, and requests are logged and managed. If data is missing or incomplete, |

## 7: *Continual value co-creation*

> it can be harder to track whether requests are being fulfilled according to agreed procedures and delivering user satisfaction. Post-request reviews can be an important source of information for this PSF.

# CHAPTER 8: REALISING AND VALIDATING SERVICE VALUE

This chapter is focused on step 7 of the customer journey: **realise**.

Key topics include:

- Methods for measuring service usage and customer and user experience and satisfaction;
- Methods to track and monitor service value;
- Different types of reporting of service outcome and performance;
- Charging mechanisms;
- How to validate service value;
- How to evaluate and improve the customer journey; and
- How the portfolio management practice can be applied to service value realisation.

This step of the customer journey is where value is tracked, assessed and evaluated. Service and customer journey improvements should be continually identified, and service value optimised. This step ensures that stakeholders achieve their desired outcomes, and related costs and risk are managed.

Service providers need to know the product or service baseline and targets in order to track, assess and evaluate service value realisation. There may be a delay between initial product and service delivery and value being realised, so this could be a long process. It is important to track when

## 8: Realising and validating service value

and where value will be realised; where will the ultimate benefit be measured?

Tracking value realisation can be expensive and time consuming. The cost and effort should be balanced against benefits, and improvements applied where possible.

*"Service value is always perceived value, which makes it difficult to track and evaluate as it is based on individual expectations and preferences. This is why tracking customer experience and satisfaction is just as important as tracking outputs and outcomes."*

Table 57 shows more information on the purpose of value capturing and customer journey improvement.

**Table 57: The Purpose of Value Capturing and Customer Journey Improvement[55]**

| *Realize* | *For the service consumer* | *For the service provider* |
|---|---|---|
| Facilitate outcome and experience | *To realize the planned value*<br><br>*To enable confirmation of value realization*<br><br>*To establish effective communication with the service provider* | *To realize value for the service provider (e.g. earn money, capability elevation, etc.)*<br><br>*To enhance feedback from the customer* |

---

[55] *ITIL® 4: Drive Stakeholder Value*, table 9.1. Copyright © AXELOS Limited 2020. Used under permission of AXELOS Limited. All rights reserved.

## 8: Realising and validating service value

|  | for providing feedback on service quality | To increase customer's involvement in service operations and improvement |
|---|---|---|
| Optimize risk and compliance | To detect deviations from the desired state in order to reallocate resources if needed | To detect deviations from the desired state before the customer satisfaction decreases<br><br>To demonstrate realized value, such as reduced risk of customer dissatisfaction |
| Optimize resources and minimize cost | To avoid inefficient allocation of resources<br><br>To increase awareness of how value is created and what the alternatives are | To avoid inefficient allocation of resources<br><br>To ensure cost covering |

**Service and value measurement and validation**

Key concepts for measurement and validation include:

- Realising service value;
- Tracking value realisation;

# 8: Realising and validating service value

- Tracking performance, output and outcome;
- Tracking experience and satisfaction;
- Tracking service usage;
- Assessing and reporting value realisation;
- Evaluating value realisation;
- Evaluation and verification;
- Continual improvement;
- Service provider goals; and
- Charging mechanisms.

## Realising service value

The type of service relationship will influence how value is tracked, assessed and evaluated. Partnerships may include joint value tracking with shared activities, whereas basic or out-of-the-box relationships may rely on standard reports.

The higher the costs and risks associated with the service, the more effort the customer is likely to put into value realisation tracking and assessment – table 58 shows more information.

# 8: Realising and validating service value

**Table 58: Tracking, Assessing, and Evaluating Value Realization In Different Types of Service Relationships**[56]

| Relationship | Basic relationship | Cooperative relationship | Partnership |
|---|---|---|---|
| Service provider | Mostly external | External or internal | External or internal |
| Services | Commercial off-the-shelf services, out-of-the-box services, cloud, or highly standardized commodity services or goods supply | Services that have to be configured or customized to fulfil the needs of the service consumer | Custom or bespoke services with unique value propositions |
| Approach for tracking and realization of value | Little interest in outcomes for the other party | The consumer mostly relies on evidence provided by the trusted service provider | The consumer and the service provider track and validate value together as partners |

---

[56] *ITIL® 4: Drive Stakeholder Value*, table 9.2. Copyright © AXELOS Limited 2020. Used under permission of AXELOS Limited. All rights reserved.

## 8: Realising and validating service value

| Relationship | Basic relationship | Cooperative relationship | Partnership |
|---|---|---|---|
| Customer activities | If service costs are comparatively low for the customer, tracking and evaluating value realization is unnecessary<br><br>If costs are high for the customer: basic value, outcome, cost, and risk (VOCR) analysis based on:<br><br>• assumptions /business case made at the offer step<br>• reports provided by the service provider | Advanced VOCR analysis based on agreement and promises agreed as part of the agree step (outcomes review, benefit realization according to benefit realization plan, analysis of side-effects and risks, cost–benefit analysis, ROI if applicable) | Same as in a cooperative relationship, but fulfilled jointly |
| Shared activities | Ad hoc service review | Joint service review of | Continual tracking and analysis of |

## 8: Realising and validating service value

| Relationship | Basic relationship | Cooperative relationship | Partnership |
|---|---|---|---|
| | | achievements compared to agreements and promises<br><br>Joint surveys and analysis of opportunities for improvement<br><br>Occasional joint experiment-ation (pilots, early access, etc.) | the outcomes, costs, and risks, and seeking optimization<br><br>Service provider and consumer data sharing and joint research<br><br>Continual experiment-ation |
| Service provider activities | Customer-oriented activities: reporting on service outputs<br><br>Service provider-oriented activities: mass market:<br>• analysis of profitability/cost-effectiveness of service | Customer-oriented activities:<br>• providing sophisticated reports on service level and KPIs related to agreed promises<br>• analysis of customer's outcomes (compared with | Same as in a cooperative relationship, but fulfilled jointly |

## 8: Realising and validating service value

| Relationship | Basic relationship | Cooperative relationship | Partnership |
|---|---|---|---|
| | delivery among large groups or all service customers<br>• providing access to reports/ analytics embedded into the service (if applicable)<br>Internal provider: risk and costs control | agreements and promises)<br>Service provider-oriented activities:<br>• analysis of profitability/<br>• cost-effectiveness of service delivery<br>• risk assessment<br>• tracking demand and forecasting future demand and relationship development | |

Service value indicators are measures *"that either directly or indirectly indicate the situation or level of a specific aspect of service value. Indicators reflect the achievement of an objective."* Service value indicators are tracked and measured to support value realisation tracking and assessment.

Indicators are supported by metrics. Tracking value realisation includes:

## 8: Realising and validating service value

- Identifying direct and indirect service value indicators and the links between them;
- Defining and measuring underpinning metrics; and
- Capturing measurement data.

Figure 23 shows the flow from purpose to metrics.

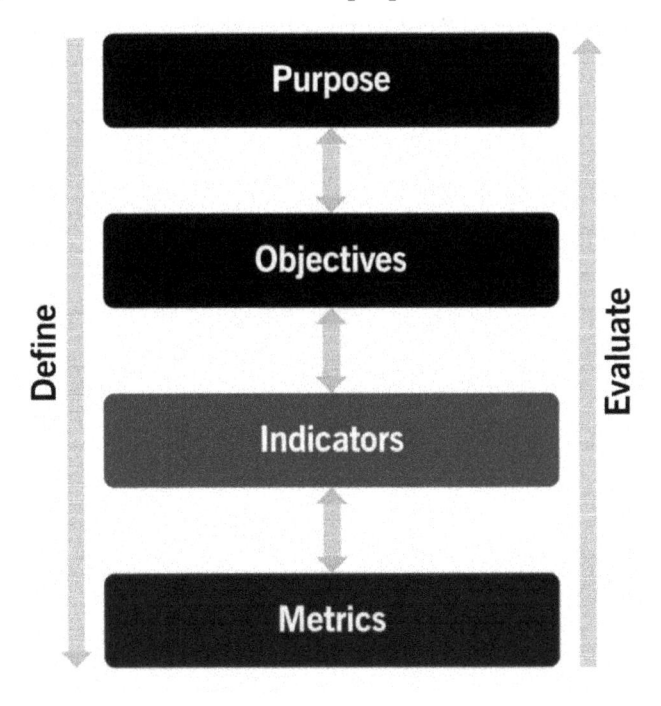

**Figure 23: ITIL planning and evaluation model**[57]

---

[57] *ITIL® 4: Drive Stakeholder Value*, figure 9.1. Copyright © AXELOS Limited 2020. Used under permission of AXELOS Limited. All rights reserved.

# 8: Realising and validating service value

## Tracking performance, output and outcome

Measuring the outcome of a service can be challenging. Many service providers measure outputs and performance to give an indirect measure of an outcome. Measuring outcomes directly can be much more challenging.

Figure 24[58] shows the service profit chain.

---

[58] *ITIL® 4: Drive Stakeholder Value*, figure 9.2. Copyright © AXELOS Limited 2020. Used under permission of AXELOS Limited. All rights reserved.

## 8: Realising and validating service value

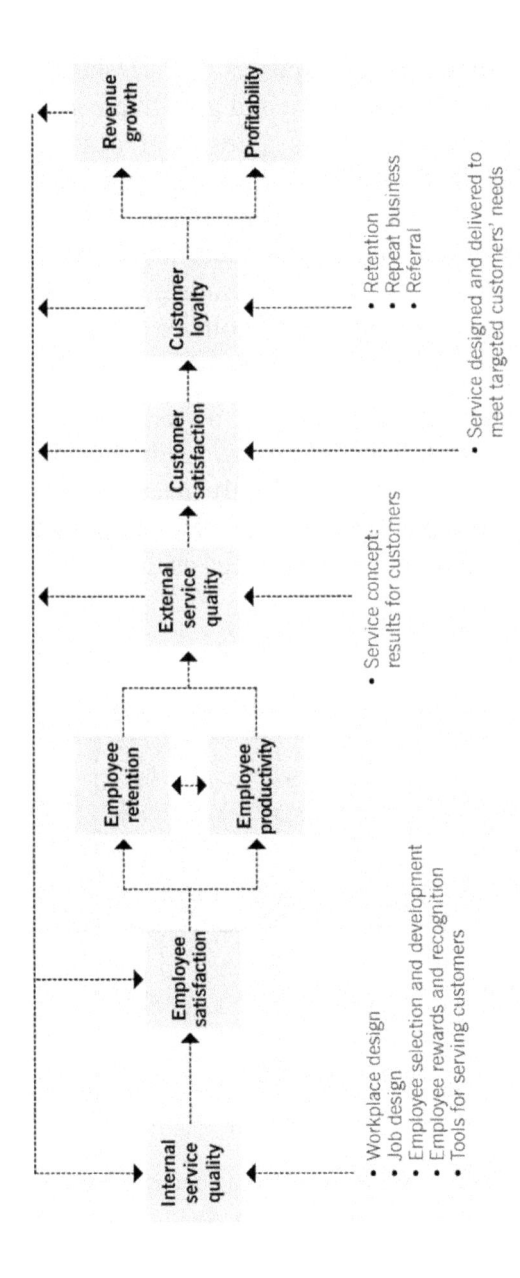

**Figure 24: The service profit chain**

## 8: Realising and validating service value

The service profit chain is a way of linking performance and outputs to outcomes, proposed by Heskett in 1994. According to the model, profit and growth are stimulated by customer loyalty. Loyalty is a result of customers being satisfied. Satisfaction is influenced by the value of the services that the customer is consuming. Value associated with services is created by satisfied, loyal and productive employees, and that employee satisfaction comes from having high-quality support and policies that deliver a good employee experience.

There are many models that can be used to link outputs, outcomes and business objectives. Each organisation will have to choose one that most closely meets its requirements. Some products will have unexpected or unintended side effects. These also need to be tracked as they could represent value generated.

Table 59 shows levels of value realisation tracking.

**Table 59: Levels of Value Realization Tracking**[59]

| *Level of value realization* | *Examples* | *Success criteria and relevant metrics* | *Related methods and practices* |
|---|---|---|---|
| Resource performance (task processing) | Work to be done by the service | Timely task processing (e.g. response | Tracking tickets and tasks |

---

[59] *ITIL® 4: Drive Stakeholder Value*, table 9.3. Copyright © AXELOS Limited 2020. Used under permission of AXELOS Limited. All rights reserved.

## 8: Realising and validating service value

| Level of value realization | Examples | Success criteria and relevant metrics | Related methods and practices |
|---|---|---|---|
| | provider, such as:<br>• service desk<br>• change enablement as a service (e.g. database administration) | time, resolution time) | See the service desk practice guide |
| Resource/ product performance (access to the IT resource) | The customer needs an IT resource or access to an IT resource or highly standardized service (e.g. email, intranet, printing service) | Resource/ product availability and performance, measured by:<br>• mean time to restore service (MTTRS), mean time between failures (MTBF)<br>• transaction volume per time period<br>• response time | IT infrastructure monitoring<br><br>See the capacity and performance management practice guide |

## 8: Realising and validating service value

| Level of value realization | Examples | Success criteria and relevant metrics | Related methods and practices |
|---|---|---|---|
| Service performance (utility and warranty) | The customer needs a service tailored to its needs. For out-of-the-box and digital services, service performance may equal product performance | Service levels against targets | SLA score boards. See the service level management practice guide |
| Consumer (organization) performance | The customer treats the service as a process enabler. For example, IT enablement of settlement and cash servicing, IT enablement of credit application | More efficient process, cheaper or fewer resources throughput per time period. Task execution time | Business transaction monitoring, real user monitoring, maturity assessment. See the capacity and performance management practice guide |

## 8: Realising and validating service value

| Level of value realization | Examples | Success criteria and relevant metrics | Related methods and practices |
|---|---|---|---|
| | processing, calendar app | The average volume of a queue | |
| Consumer (strategic) objectives | The customer need for the service is used as a tool for achieving the strategic objective, resulting in:<br><br>• better quality<br>• introduction of new products or services<br>• improved customer retention<br><br>Examples include CRM and internet banking | Achieving strategic objectives<br><br>Consumer metrics depending on an objective | Post-implementation review, business intelligence analytics<br><br>See the project management practice guide |

## 8: Realising and validating service value

| Level of value realization | Examples | Success criteria and relevant metrics | Related methods and practices |
|---|---|---|---|
| Consumer purpose (profitability) | The customer treats service acquisitions as investments; choosing services for consumption is a portfolio decision | Achieving financial goals such as ROI, NPV, internal rate of return, etc., against targets<br><br>Achieving non-financial goals | Return on investment evaluation<br><br>See the portfolio management practice guide<br><br>Tracking attitude, behaviour, culture changes<br><br>See the organizational change management practice guide |
| Consumer purpose (risk mitigation) | The customer treats the service as a risk mitigation measure | Effective and efficient risk mitigation:<br>• residual risk: actual against projected<br>• losses: actual | Risk assessment, business impact analysis<br><br>See the risk management practice guide |

## 8: Realising and validating service value

| Level of value realization | Examples | Success criteria and relevant metrics | Related methods and practices |
|---|---|---|---|
|  |  | against expected |  |

\* *All relevant data (staff reductions or efficiency improvements, improvements in business performance, quality measurements, etc.) should be converted to monetary values and then compared to service costs.*

Quantitative and qualitative measures should be applied to value realisation tracking:

- Quantitative means 'relating to, measuring, or measured by the quantity of something rather than its quality'.
- Qualitative means 'relating to, measuring, or measured by the quality of something rather than its quantity'.

Some elements of value cannot be measured quantitatively but are still important to track. For example, better knowledge leading to better capabilities could be tracked qualitatively.

### *Tracking experience and satisfaction*

To get a holistic view of customer and user satisfaction, service providers should:

- Measure and track customer and user experience;
- Perform customer and user satisfaction surveys; and
- Request and process feedback from service consumers.

Table 60 shows tracking examples.

## 8: Realising and validating service value

**Table 60: Tracking Service Experience and Satisfaction**[60]

| Experience criteria | Experience characteristic | Metrics |
|---|---|---|
| Functional experience<br><br>How does the service work? | Uninterrupted completion of user actions | Number and frequency of user errors<br><br>Frequency of returns to the previous stage ('back-button usage')<br><br>Number and frequency of dropped (unfinished) service actions |
| Emotional experience<br><br>How does the service feel? | Clear and convenient interface<br><br>Effortlessness and speed of service actions completion | Number and percentage of transactions where users used the interface help<br><br>Average handling time (the average duration of one |

---

[60] *ITIL® 4: Drive Stakeholder Value*, table 9.4. Copyright © AXELOS Limited 2020. Used under permission of AXELOS Limited. All rights reserved.

## 8: Realising and validating service value

| Experience criteria | Experience characteristic | Metrics |
|---|---|---|
| | | transaction from the customer's call to ticket resolution) |
| | | *Customer effort score measures customer satisfaction (how much effort customers have to put into getting their issues solved using the service)* |
| | | *First response rate (the average time it takes for a support agent to respond to a customer)* |
| | | *Average and minimum rating given by users about service interface* |
| *Satisfaction*<br><br>*To what degree does the service fulfil needs?* | *The reflection of functional and emotional experiences* | *Average and minimum rating given by users to the service* |

## 8: Realising and validating service value

| Experience criteria | Experience characteristic | Metrics |
|---|---|---|
| | that indicates the level of satisfaction while using the service and loyalty to the service provider | Number and percentage of users who cancel subscription after a trial period<br><br>Customer churn rate (percentage of customers that stopped using the service during a timeframe)<br><br>Net promoter score measures customer loyalty (percentage of customers who are promoters of an organization or service) |

Customer and user experience can be tracked by asking:

- How does the service work? This measures the functional experience.
- How does the service feel? This measures the emotional experience.
- To what degree does the service fulfil your needs? This measures satisfaction.

## 8: Realising and validating service value

Service providers need to correlate experience data with service performance data. If there is a mismatch (for example, very low customer satisfaction but the service has been available and working), this may highlight a wider issue. Service level metrics can be used to support this correlation.

### Tracking service usage

Service usage analytics and service metering help to track, map and understand customer and user behaviour. The service provider can use this information and patterns of business activity to ensure services will be able to match levels of demand.

### Assessing and reporting value realisation

Customers will want information about service outcomes from the service provider. This will include areas such as:

- Return on investment
- Achievement of strategic objectives
- Process performance
- Satisfaction
- Service levels
- Etc.

These levels are all connected, and the customer and service provider need to work together to build meaningful information.

Assessing and reporting value realisation includes gathering and consolidating data from different sources. Information needs to be interpreted and assessed and presented in a way that supports decision making. Data capture ranges from

## 8: Realising and validating service value

formal service reviews to informal meetings and discussions. Once captured, data can be correlated with outcomes, risks and costs.

Table 61 shows two levels of reporting on value realisation.

**Table 61: Two Levels of Assessing and Reporting On Value Realization[61]**

|  | *Assessing and reporting on experience, performance, and output data* | *Assessing and reporting outcomes, risks, and costs* |
|---|---|---|
| Procedure | *Relate the captured experience, performance and output data to agreement targets (if applicable)*<br><br>*Combine data using proper techniques*<br><br>*Build reports using agreed report templates or dashboards* | *Correlate experience, performance, and output data with service outcomes, risks, and costs*<br><br>*Link service experience, outcome, risks, and costs with service consumer objectives and* |

---

[61] *ITIL® 4: Drive Stakeholder Value*, table 9.5. Copyright © AXELOS Limited 2020. Used under permission of AXELOS Limited. All rights reserved.

## 8: Realising and validating service value

|  | Assessing and reporting on experience, performance, and output data | Assessing and reporting outcomes, risks, and costs |
|---|---|---|
|  |  | purposes using mapping tools |
| Data aggregation and correlation techniques | IT component to scorecard hierarchy | Organizational improvement cascade or similar |
| Assessment and reporting methods | SLA scorecard<br><br>Service level reports and dashboards<br><br>Service reviews | Return on investment evaluation<br><br>Cost–benefit analysis (including outcomes, costs, and risks)<br><br>Post-implementation review, retrospectives, audits, and more<br><br>Benchmarking |

## 8: Realising and validating service value

|  | *Assessing and reporting on experience, performance, and output data* | *Assessing and reporting outcomes, risks, and costs* |
|---|---|---|
| Relevant ITIL practices | Capacity and performance management<br><br>Measurement and reporting<br><br>Risk management (provides risk data)<br><br>Service financial management (provides cost data)<br><br>Service level management | Portfolio management<br><br>Relationship management<br><br>Risk management (provides risk data)<br><br>Service financial management (provides cost data) |

Data analysis includes asking questions such as:

- Are targets being met?
- Are there any clear trends (positive or negative)?
- Are any improvements required?
- Are there any significant underlying issues?
- Are there any unexpected patterns or outcomes? Do they need to be fed back to service design and improvement?
- Is there any new contextual information (products, services, customer journey, market)?

# 8: Realising and validating service value

## *Evaluating value realisation*

Evaluating value realisation verifies that services have created the desired value and that the desired customer experience has been achieved. This is 'single loop' learning. 'Double loop' learning builds on this to check if the original value proposition is still valid, and that the service value system is fit for purpose.

## *Evaluation and verification*

Simple services are relatively easy to evaluate. If targets are being met, everything is working as it should. In more complex environments, evaluation cannot be fully formalised. The service provider and consumer need to work together (for example, in service reviews) to evaluate value realisation.

Targets will change and evolve over time, so these changes need to be captured during the evaluation and verification process.

Evaluation allows assumptions to be challenged. Ask questions including:

- Is there still a problem that needs to be solved?
- Is the service still the best way to solve the problem?
- Is the service still fit for purpose and fit for use?

The customer must keep the service provider informed about changes that may affect the service and its outcomes, experience, costs and risks.

## *Continual improvement*

Evaluation of value realisation supports continual improvement. Other sources of improvement data include:

## 8: Realising and validating service value

- Service usage analytics;
- Analysis of service request patterns;
- Incidents, complaints, problems;
- Change and improvement requests; and
- User feedback.

Continual improvement could include improvements to the service, product, or any element of the service value system. These ITIL practices enable continual improvement through their information:

- Incident management
- Knowledge management
- Monitoring and event management
- Service catalogue management
- Service desk
- Service request management

> Banksbest interacts with its customers in different ways, including in branches, via the customer service centre and via its online services. How can each channel support improvement activities? What type of data can it provide?

### Service provider goals

The service provider also has value realisation goals, and it will use the same techniques as the customer to track them.

## 8: Realising and validating service value

**Internal service providers** share the same strategic goals as the legal entity that 'owns' them. An internal service provider does not have its own business goals. It exists to facilitate value for customers and users. The service provider will track its own outcomes, but these will usually be incorporated into the wider tracking, assessment and evaluation of customer outcomes.

**External service providers** have their own business goals. Helping its customers achieve their goals should help the service provider to achieve its own goals. These goals could include financial, brand recognition, market share, resource use, capability elevation, etc. The external service provider needs to track its own value realisation in addition to customer value realisation.

### *Charging mechanisms*

For a service provider, value realisation includes profit or cost recovery. Charging policies can include:

- Cost recovery (break-even) – the service provider recovers its costs and doesn't make a profit or a loss;
- Recovery with margin – the service provider makes a margin (not a profit) that is reinvested into services;
- Cross-subsidisation – the margin from one service is used to subsidise another service; and
- Profit – the service provider aims to make a profit.

Internal service provider prices are normally based on costs. Chargeable items can be used to define costs. Chargeable items describe a cost unit from the customer's perspective. Organisations with internal service providers need to balance the time and resources used for internal charging against the

# 8: Realising and validating service value

benefits of the process; for example, does it influence behaviour?

Charging describes the process for recovering money from the customer. Billing is how the invoice is produced and presented. Billing options include:

- No billing – if costs are covered via enterprise cost allocation;
- Informational billing or show-back – an invoice is produced but for information only;
- Internal billing or chargeback – internal customers receive a bill (or cross-charge) for their service usage; and
- Billing and collection – this will be supported by a financial system tracking invoicing, collection, debtors and creditors.

## The portfolio management practice

A portfolio is a collection of assets into which an organisation chooses to invest its resources in order to receive the best return.

The purpose of the portfolio management practice is *"to ensure that the organization has the right mix of programs, projects, products, and services to execute the organization's strategy within its funding and resource constraints"*.

Portfolio management helps to track and realise value for the service provider by:

- Identifying investment with the highest payoff; and
- Analysing and tracking investments.

## 8: Realising and validating service value

It enables single and double loop learning and can provide a snapshot of the current state of investment, as well as formal assessment reports.

There are several types of portfolios.

**Product and service portfolio:**
*"The complete set of products and services that are managed by the organization, representing the organization's commitments and investments across all of its customers and market spaces. This portfolio also represents current contractual commitments, new product and service development, and ongoing improvement plans."*

**Project portfolio:**
*"Used to manage and coordinate projects, ensuring that objectives are met within time and cost constraints and to their specifications. The project portfolio also ensures that projects are not duplicated and stay within the agreed scope, and that resources are available for each project. This portfolio is used to manage single projects as well as large-scale programs. It supports the organization's product and service portfolio and improvements to the organization's practices and service value system (SVS)."*

**Customer portfolio:**
*"This portfolio reflects the organization's commitment to serving certain consumer groups and market spaces. It may influence the structure and content of the product and service portfolio and the project portfolio. The customer portfolio is*

## 8: Realising and validating service value

used to ensure that the relationship between business outcomes, customers, and services is well understood."

Portfolios can be used to manage resources (for example customers, applications or suppliers). The purpose is to achieve optimal return on the investment and use of the assets. Portfolio management is closely related to many different practices, but none more so than the service financial management practice. As portfolio management ensures fiscal management (when to invest, how to invest, etc.), costing, value propositions, and other data from service financial management are crucial.

A value proposition is *"an explicit promise made by a service provider to its customers that it will deliver a particular bundle of benefits"*.

### Practice success factors

There are two practice success factors for portfolio management. They are:

*"Ensuring sound investment decisions for programs, projects, products, and services within the organization's resource constraints*

*Ensuring the continual monitoring, review, and optimization of the organization's portfolios"*

**Table 62: PSF: Ensure Sound Investment Decisions Within Resource Constraints**

| PSF: Ensure sound investment decisions within resource constraints |
|---|
| As organisations grow or change their focus, the many possible initiatives can create conflicting priorities. The |

## 8: Realising and validating service value

portfolio management practice ensures that the stakeholder view is included in the prioritisation activities so that more important initiatives are provided with the necessary resources before less important initiatives.

All portfolio entries are assessed against the organisational strategy, understanding the value and risk propositions. The assessment criteria and how they are applied should be transparent and consistent. The financial valuation of each possible initiative is provided by the service financial management practice, and the organisational strategy is communicated by the organisational leadership and the strategy management practice.

Portfolios focus on the prioritisation and re-prioritisation activities of an organisation, ensuring product and service activities provide the necessary value proposition. Additionally, as portfolios get larger, there should be a named owner to ensure the necessary information is captured, updated and shared, as required. The use of a portfolio to manage investment decisions should be clearly communicated to all decision-makers in the organisation. This keeps the method and application of prioritisation consistent and transparent.

**Table 63: PSF: Ensure Continual Monitoring, Review and Optimisation of Portfolios**

| PSF: Ensure continual monitoring, review and optimisation of portfolios |
|---|
| While initiatives are prioritised based on projected value, the potential value delivery needs to be monitored and assessed against original value proposition. If the product |

## 8: Realising and validating service value

or service is providing the necessary value, that item remains in the portfolio. If the product or service fails to deliver the promised value, then that item needs to be improved or removed from the portfolio.

Note: items may provide the necessary value proposition but no longer meet the strategic needs of the organisation, and those products and services would also be removed from the portfolio.

The portfolio owner should review their portfolio regularly and provide a 'heath check' report. This report should capture the value realised from each portfolio item. For ease, create a template and use it across all portfolios. Compare the results of the assessment to predetermined criteria. Based on the findings from the assessment of the portfolio, new initiatives or improvement efforts are the typical outcome. The change enablement practice will provide guidance on how to manage those actions as well as the decision to retire or remove products or services from the portfolio.

# CHAPTER 9: EXAM PREPARATION

**Here are the key facts about the ITIL 4 Specialist: Drive Stakeholder Value exam:**

The exam is 90 minutes. Extra time is allowable if English is not your native language and a translated paper isn't available.

- The exam is closed book – it's just you and your knowledge.
- It has 40 multiple-choice questions, and you must get 28 correct, or 70% to pass.
- There is no negative marking (so you don't lose a mark if you get a question wrong).
- There are 13 questions at Bloom's Level 2 and 27 at Bloom's Level 3.
- Remember that this course is part of the Managing Professional stream.

Your training provider for ITIL 4 Specialist: Drive Stakeholder Value certification will provide you with access to at least one sample exam. When you're ready to attempt the sample paper, try to reproduce, as far as possible, the conditions of the real exam.

Set aside 90 minutes to complete the paper and make sure there are no distractions: don't make a coffee; don't raid the refrigerator; don't check your emails … or Facebook … or Twitter; switch off your phone.

If you don't focus exclusively on the sample exam questions, you will not have a good indication of your possible

## 9: Exam preparation

performance in the live exam. Your sample exam may highlight areas for further study before you take your final exam.

*9: Exam preparation*

**Here are some good practices for taking multiple-choice exams:**

**Manage your time:** if you're stuck on a question, mark it and go back to it later. It's easy to spend too long staring at one question, but there may be easier marks to be picked up further on in the paper.

**Have a technique:** I like to go through an exam and complete all the questions I feel confident about. That allows me to see how many of the more challenging ones I need to get right to have a successful result.

**Trust your instinct:** one of the most common bits of exam feedback is delegates who wish they had not changed their answer at the last minute. It's fine to check over what you've done, but be very wary about making changes in those last few seconds.

**Use the process of elimination:** each question has four possible answers – if you can discount one or two of them, then you've dramatically increased your odds of picking the right answer.

**Don't panic!** If your mind goes blank, move on, and look at another question – you can do this with online and paper exams. Your subconscious mind will work away even when you're answering a different question.

## 9: Exam preparation

> **Read the question carefully:** if you're not careful, you will answer the question you think you see, not the one that's actually there.

And that's all from me! I hope you've enjoyed the book, and that the extra content I've provided along the way will help you start using ITIL 4 DSV concepts in your own role. You can find me on LinkedIn and Twitter – I'd love to hear if you've enjoyed the book and how your studies and your exam help you in your career.

- *www.linkedin.com/in/claireagutter/*
- *https://twitter.com/ClaireAgutter*

# APPENDIX A: BANKSBEST CASE STUDY

**Company overview**

Banksbest was originally HW Banking. It was founded in 1953 in the UK and has branches in most major UK cities. It focuses mainly on business clients, but it also has a mortgage department that offers residential mortgages to aspiring homeowners and buy-to-let mortgages to landlords.

The Banksbest board of directors initiated a digital transformation programme in 2017. At the same time, a new CEO and CIO were recruited. A Chief Digital Officer (CDO) role has also been established. As part of the digital transformation programme, the bank rebranded from HW Banking to Banksbest, which was seen as a more customer-focused brand.

Banksbest has defined these strategic goals:

- To be the tenth largest provider of business banking services in the UK (growing its customer base by approximately 25%).
- To grow its residential mortgage business by 50%.
- To build a reputation as a 'digital first' banking provider.

There is some conflict during board meetings, as the CFO is not fully convinced about the value of the CDO role and the digital transformation programme. She would prefer to focus on cost management.

The head office and data centre for Banksbest are in Manchester. The customer service centre is in Reading. There is also an agreement with a business process

*Appendix A: Banksbest case study*

outsourcing company in Bulgaria, Employeez on Demand, which provides additional customer service resources during peak times. The customer service centre operates 7 days a week, between 8:00 am and 6:00 pm, and support is also available via the bank's website on a 24x7 basis.

Banksbest's 50 branches are open Monday to Saturday, between 9:00 am and 5:00 pm.

Banksbest has a good reputation in a competitive field. However, the rebrand has confused some customers, and the digital transformation programme has not delivered many measurable results yet. Banksbest needs to improve its online services and embed its new brand in order to grow.

**Company structure**

Banksbest employs 700 staff. 400 work in the bank's branches, 100 in the call centre, and 200 in the head office and support functions. Additional staff are supplied by Employeez on Demand during peak times.

Banksbest is split into divisions:

- Central Operations – provides support services for all departments. Operations includes HR, Finance, Marketing and IT. The IT department has 50 staff.
- Customer Services – this department includes the staff who work in and manage the customer service centre, as well as technical specialists who work on the systems used in the CS centre.
- Branches – this department is responsible for the branches providing face-to-face banking services. The branches are expensive to maintain but offer a face-to-face service that some Banksbest customers value.

*Appendix A: Banksbest case study*

The digital transformation programme is being run by a digital team that operates outside the existing divisions.

**Future plans**

To achieve its goals, Banksbest and the digital transformation programme team are working on different initiatives. These include the flagship 'My Way' project, which will allow business banking customers to access services however suits them best. Commissioned by the CDO and led by a product owner, My Way will allow business banking customers to use a range of devices to manage their accounts and move seamlessly between branch-based and online transactions. The current plans include:

- Testing biometrics including fingerprint and voice login to support My Way;
- My Deposit My Way, allowing cheques to be paid in using the camera on a mobile phone; and
- Monitoring of customer feedback, levels of demand and which products are most popular.

After three months, the product owner will report back to the CDO. At this point, the project will either be allocated additional funding, will pivot, or will be closed down. My Way is being measured on both governance and compliance and customer satisfaction outcomes.

**IT services**

All the IT services are run from the head office and the Manchester data centre. Since the digital transformation programme started, more services are Cloud hosted by external providers. The main IT services are:

*Appendix A: Banksbest case study*

**Bizbank** – the banking system used in the branches and customer service centre. This system contains customer account information and history, including current and savings accounts. Bizbank is hosted in the Manchester data centre, but there are plans to move it to a Cloud hosting service to improve its resilience. Bizbank incidents sometimes take a long time to resolve because the original developers have left, and documentation is poor.

**Mortbank** – the mortgage system used in branches and the customer service centre. As well as tracking existing mortgages, Mortbank has a credit-checking facility that supports mortgage approvals. Mortbank was developed by MortSys, which provides ongoing support and maintenance. MortSys is a small organisation and doesn't always respond within its agreed target times.

**Mibank** – an online self-service portal being developed as part of the My Way project. Mibank allows customers to check their accounts, move money between accounts, pay bills and receive cheques. The functionality of Mibank will expand as the My Way project progresses.

**Banksec** – Banksec is an identity-checking utility that is used by Bizbank, Mortbank and Mibank. Banksec uses two-factor authentication, and biometric capabilities are in development.

## IT department

The IT department includes 50 staff split into 4 departments, under the CIO:

- Strategic Planning and Business Relationship Management.
- Service Management.

*Appendix A: Banksbest case study*

- Development.
- Operations (including Service Desk).

IT has a good reputation generally, but business staff see the IT department as responsible for day-to-day operations and fixing things. The IT department's development role is less well understood. There is also friction between the digital transformation programme staff and IT staff.

**IT service management**

Service management does not have a high profile in Banksbest.

The CIO holds a position at board level, and likes to be seen as dynamic and responsive, rather than process driven and bureaucratic. However, recent service outages have led to a level of interest in service management best practices, as well as assessment of other ways of working including DevOps, Agile and Lean.

There are culture issues in the IT department, including an 'us and them' attitude that means developers and operations staff don't always work well together.

### Sample employee biographies

| | |
|---|---|
| **Lucy Jones** | Lucy joined Banksbest as a graduate trainee five years ago. As part of her training, she spent six months in each of the major departments: Central Operations, Branches and Customer Services. During her time in Central Operations, she spent two months in Finance, two months in HR and two months in IT, including working on the Service Desk. |

*Appendix A: Banksbest case study*

|  | |
|---|---|
|  | Following completion of her graduate trainee programme, Lucy was offered a job in HR, and worked there for three years. She was then offered a newly created role of Product Owner and is responsible for the 'My Way' project. Lucy has a good understanding of the Banksbest business units and the IT services that support them. |
| **Doug Range** | Doug has worked for Banksbest for 20 years since it was HW Banking. He started work as counter staff in one of the branches and worked his way up to branch manager. Some years ago, his branch was chosen to be one of the pilot locations for the rollout of Bizbank, and for two years he acted as a super-user for this system, logging the queries he handled on the service desk system. He has recently been promoted to a head office role, including training the customer service centre staff.<br><br>Doug is working with Lucy on the My Way project, helping to provide customer intelligence, and ensuring the customer service centre staff are kept up to date. |

# FURTHER READING

IT Governance Publishing (ITGP) is the world's leading publisher for governance and compliance. Our industry-leading pocket guides, books, training resources and toolkits are written by real-world practitioners and thought leaders. They are used globally by audiences of all levels, from students to C-suite executives.

Our high-quality publications cover all IT governance, risk and compliance frameworks and are available in a range of formats. This ensures our customers can access the information they need in the way they need it.

Other ITIL publications by Claire Agutter include:

- *ITIL® 4 Essentials – Your essential guide for the ITIL 4 Foundation exam and beyond, second edition*, www.itgovernancepublishing.co.uk/product/itil-4-essentials-your-essential-guide-for-the-itil-4-foundation-exam-and-beyond-second-edition
- *ITIL® 4 Direct, Plan and Improve (DPI) – Your companion to the ITIL 4 Managing Professional and Strategic Leader DPI certification*, www.itgovernancepublishing.co.uk/product/itil-4-direct-plan-and-improve-dpi
- *ITIL® 4 High-velocity IT (HVIT) – Your companion to the ITIL 4 Managing Professional HVIT certification*, www.itgovernancepublishing.co.uk/product/itil-4-high-velocity-it-hvit

## Further reading

- *ITIL® 4 Create, Deliver and Support (CDS) – Your companion to the ITIL 4 Managing Professional CDS certification*, www.itgovernancepublishing.co.uk/product/itil-4-create-deliver-and-support-cds

For more information on ITGP and branded publishing services, and to view our full list of publications, visit www.itgovernancepublishing.co.uk.

To receive regular updates from ITGP, including information on new publications in your area(s) of interest, sign up for our newsletter at www.itgovernancepublishing.co.uk/topic/newsletter.

### Branded publishing

Through our branded publishing service, you can customise ITGP publications with your company's branding.

Find out more at www.itgovernancepublishing.co.uk/topic/branded-publishing-services.

### Related services

ITGP is part of GRC International Group, which offers a comprehensive range of complementary products and services to help organisations meet their objectives.

For a full range of resources on ITIL visit www.itgovernance.co.uk/shop/category/itil.

### Training services

The IT Governance training programme is built on our extensive practical experience designing and implementing management systems based on ISO standards, best practice and regulations.

Our courses help attendees develop practical skills and comply with contractual and regulatory requirements. They also support career development via recognised qualifications.

Learn more about our training courses in ITIL and view the full course catalogue at *www.itgovernance.co.uk/training*.

**Professional services and consultancy**

We are a leading global consultancy of IT governance, risk management and compliance solutions. We advise businesses around the world on their most critical issues and present cost-saving and risk-reducing solutions based on international best practice and frameworks.

We offer a wide range of delivery methods to suit all budgets, timescales and preferred project approaches.

Find out how our consultancy services can help your organisation at *www.itgovernance.co.uk/consulting*.

**Industry news**

Want to stay up to date with the latest developments and resources in the IT governance and compliance market? Subscribe to our Weekly Round-up newsletter and we will send you mobile-friendly emails with fresh news and features about your preferred areas of interest, as well as unmissable offers and free resources to help you successfully start your projects. *www.itgovernance.co.uk/weekly-round-up*.

Lightning Source UK Ltd.
Milton Keynes UK
UKHW021048150222
398722UK00005B/185